"In his inimitable way, Roberts describes how the rhetorical patter talk about free-markets is a cover story for the horror of an extractive asset-stripping operation by publicly-supported private banks and the governments that they control that impoverishes people and the environment. He shows that unrealistic assumptions made by free-trade ideologues have led to the "New Dispossession" and a political and economic race to the bottom, applauded as a success story by junk economists, who ignore the reductions in living standards and rise in environmental instability.

Roberts describes how Germany's economic surplus is being used to serve private European financial predators, and how the highly touted "foreign investment in America" consists of the use of credit and trade surpluses that foreign countries have with the import-dependent US to finance the foreign purchase of the US economy, rather than to provide new capital formation that would re-employ Americans dispossessed by jobs offshoring."

MICHAEL HUDSON

"*The Failure of Laissez Faire Capitalism* is fearless. It transcends Roberts' illustrious career and prior works of intellectual and practical analysis. We are at the crossroads of a crumbling world where both policies and ideologies have failed. Roberts shows the dangers of clinging to the idea that markets are free and to the belief that unrestrained and unregulated capitalism is positive. Jobs offshoring destroyed middle class prospects, and financial deregulation fostered a rapacious banking industry that has removed itself from market discipline and threatens Western economies with collapse. Roberts' conclusions are sobering, his solutions bold, his book a compelling gift."

NOMI PRINS

THE FAILURE OF
LAISSEZ FAIRE CAPITALISM

THE FAILURE OF LAISSEZ FAIRE CAPITALISM AND ECONOMIC DISSOLUTION OF THE WEST

TOWARDS A NEW ECONOMICS FOR A FULL WORLD

PAUL CRAIG ROBERTS

CLARITY PRESS, INC.

In-house editor: Diana G. Collier
Cover: Ryan McCullough and Hudson Atwell (front cover)
and R. Jordan P. Santos

Library of Congress Cataloging-in-Publication Data

Roberts, Paul Craig, 1939-
  [Wirtschaft am Abgrund. English]
  The failure of laissez faire capitalism and economic dissolution of the West
: towards a new economics for a full world / by Paul Craig Roberts. -- first
English print
      pages cm
  ISBN 978-0-9860362-5-5
  1. Globalization--Economic aspects. 2. Capitalism. 3. Economics. I. Title.

HF1359.R58313 2013
330.12'2--dc23

                        2013020253

Clarity Press, Inc.
Ste. 469, 3277 Roswell Rd. NE
Atlanta, GA. 30305 , USA
http://www.claritypress.com

TABLE OF CONTENTS

PREFACE TO THE EUROPEAN EDITION
BY JOHANNES MARUSCHZIK / 11
    Regulation vs Deregulation / 13
    The Error of Free Trade / 14
    From Crony Capitalism to Plutocracy / 16
    How Much Longer Reserve Currency? / 18
    Quo Vadis Europe? / 20
    The End of the European National States / 24
    Critique of the Growth Model / 28

INTRODUCTION / 31

PART ONE: PROBLEMS IN ECONOMIC THEORY / 35
    Microeconomics / 36
    Macroeconomics / 37
    Free Trade Error / 47
    Offshoring Exports Jobs Instead of Products / 51
    The Problem of External Costs / 57
    Nature's Capital / 65
    Planning for a Full World / 71
    Failures of Economic Theory Are Pervasive / 75
    The Failure of Laissez Faire Capitalism / 78

PART TWO: THE NEW DISPOSSESSION / 83
    Political Dispossession / 84
    Economic Dispossession / 94
    Social Dispossession / 97
    Offshoring Displaced First World Americans / 99
    The Evidence from the Bureau of Labor Statistics / 105
    The Myth of Benevolent Globalism / 117
    Dissenters from the Myth of Benevolent Globalism / 127
    The Decimated American Economy / 131
    Unemployment / 132
    Inflation / 133

Gross Domestic Product / 133
US Wealth and Income Distribution / 134
Lies That Killed The American Dream: The Science
    and Technology Skills Shortage Myth / 135
Where Did the Money Go? / 144
Fraud by Banksters / 146
The Conflict of Interest That Masquerades
    as Government / 150
Death by Globalism / 154

PART THREE: THE END OF SOVEREIGNTY / 159
    The Undeclared Agenda / 165
    Can Germany Remain a Sovereign Country? / 171

CONCLUSION / 173

APPENDIX / 175

ENDNOTES / 180

INDEX / 184

BIO: PAUL CRAIG ROBERTS / 192

PREFACE TO THE GERMAN EDITION*

BY

JOHANNES MARUSCHZIK

We are witnesses to a historical turning point. A new world order is emerging. Economic power is shifting to the BRIC states[1] and to other emerging countries at an enormous pace. New alliances such as the Shanghai Cooperation Organisation (SCO) with China and Russia as driving forces have been preparing the new economic world order well in advance. It is very likely that they will dominate it.

However, the forces that have been leading the global economy throughout the past decades—the U.S., UK, Euroland, and Japan—are struggling to survive. Their economies are in a process of disintegration. Especially in the U.S. and in EU countries more and more people are living in poverty. Further significant losses in welfare are looming ahead. Major parts of these populations do not see any future for themselves in the global economy. Because of debt and unemployment, many states face political chaos. There is risk that radical political forces will arise from the weakness of the political and economic system and create a new form of tyranny.

Economists share the responsibility for the decline of the economies of the Western World. Rather than impartially

*This is the Preface to the German edition, published in July 2012 by Weltbuch Verlag in Germany, Austria, and Switzerland under the title, *Wirtschaft Am Abgrund*. Johannes Maruschzik is a German economist and president of the Glasshouse Center.

analysing the changes in the global world economy in order to develop responses, the different economic schools are slaves to their ideologies. Frequently, what does not fit into the theory is neglected. Furthermore, many economists are corrupted by service to interest groups and politicians who misuse the democratic system for their own purposes. By contrast, economists carrying out real scientific work are rare. They are hardly heard by policymakers.

These are key issues raised in this book by Dr. Paul Craig Roberts, who in the early stages of the government of U.S. president Ronald Reagan as Assistant Secretary of the Treasury was responsible for the economic policy of the United States.[2] This book is a fundamental challenge both analytically and empirically to economic theory and policy as presently understood and practiced.

Part 1 reviews the successes and failures of economics to the present time. It spares neither Keynesian economists, who are convinced that governments must have a big say, nor neoliberal and libertarian economists, who refuse any regulation of markets by governments. After reading the first sentences it becomes clear that the book is written by an independent, thinker who is not afraid to question conventional wisdom.

Paul Craig Roberts is closer to the libertarians than to those who think governments must run the economy. As Father of Reaganomics[3] he brought into economic policy the insight that fiscal policy shifts the aggregate supply curve, not merely the aggregate demand curve as Keynesian macroeconomics taught. High tax rates discourage work and saving and thus reduce the response of supply to policies that stimulate demand. The "Agenda 2010" of the red-green German government including cuts of the marginal tax rates would have been unthinkable without the changes that took place in the U.S. tax policy in the early 1980s and which were promoted by Paul Craig Roberts.

"Libertarians think that human nature changes according to whether it is employed privately or publicly. They don't accept that private power can be just as abusive as public power. I appreciate libertarians' defence of liberty, but I have otherwise lost patience with them." Paul Craig Roberts wrote to me these sentences at the time we were discussing the translation of this book. They link seamlessly to the warning Nobel laureate Friedrich August von Hayek expressed in his classic, *The Road to Serfdom* in 1944: "Probably nothing has done so much harm to the liberal cause as the wooden insistence of some liberals on certain rules of thumb, above all the principle of laissez-faire."[4]

In Paul Craig Roberts' eyes Laissez-faire capitalism is problematic in three areas: Firstly, the author criticises as naive the belief that markets are self-regulating. Markets are social institutions. It is the human actors in markets that require regulating. Secondly, he brings home to us that the unconditional belief in the benefits of free trade in the age of globalism must cause significant welfare losses and spread pauperism among the population not only in some developing countries but also in the Western World. Thirdly, he bemoans the ignorance of many economists that man-made capital is not a substitute for nature's capital and that the exhaustion of nature's capital in behalf of short-term profit is at the expense of future generations.

Regulation vs Deregulation

Paul Craig Roberts sees deregulation of the U.S. financial markets as the main cause of the most recent global financial and economic crisis. Alan Greenspan, chairman of the U.S. central bank, the Federal Reserve, preached the belief that markets are self-regulating. Around the millennium laws were abolished in the U.S. that had been created in light of the experiences with the Great Depression in the 1930s.[5] New highly risky and speculative financial instruments were left unregulated, and the Glass-Steagall Act was repealed, thus allowing the merging of commercial and investment banking. Experts had warned against the dangers of deregulated financial markets, especially the derivatives[6] (especially credit default swaps / CDS[7]). The warnings were ignored. The financial markets were turned into a gambling casino by the pursuit of instant riches.

We can glean information on the excesses in the U.S. financial markets in a number of books in great detail. A nightmarish subject matter that is more typical for crime novels. With a crucial difference: this is not about fiction. Rather, here was criminal energy at work that destroyed the life of millions of unsuspecting and surely also clueless people.

Paul Craig Roberts brings up a painful subject. Private power was abused on a grand scale.

The politics of deregulation opened up the opportunity and allowed an unprecedented concentration of power in the financial sector. He writes: "The economic and financial mess in which the US and Europe find themselves and which has been exported to much of the rest of the world is the direct consequence of too much economic freedom."

The Error of Free Trade

Also, on the subject of free trade the author breaks down walls: David Ricardo's free-trade theory was tightly tied to certain premises. In a globalized economy this theory has no validity. The practice of companies relocating their production of goods and services for their home markets in low-wage countries for profit reasons only (offshoring) has nothing to do with free trade. Offshoring is nothing else but labor arbitrage between differently developed countries. In the offshoring countries the jobs, the incomes, and the basis of existence that were previously related with the production disappear. Hence, fewer employees are paying taxes and contributions to social security. At the same time the number of people who need support from the state increases. By offshoring jobs, companies impose social costs on society.

Most anti-globalists criticize the exploitation of the developing countries. They do not recognize the fact that the developed industrial countries are among the main losers of globalism. The change towards a service society that has been promoted by apologists for globalism proved to be a fatal delusion.[8] Nations can create wealth only with products and services they are able to sell in the global markets. This fact was forgotten.

Paul Craig Roberts warned against the consequences of offshoring. In part 2 of his book he delivers the depressing facts on the poor prospects for the US economy.

We Europeans would be well-advised to scrutinize the development in the U.S. Isn't deindustrialization already spreading on the European continent? Isn't deindustrialization one reason for the extremely high unemployment (of young people) in the southern European countries? On balance, manufacturing has been cutting jobs also in Germany. The German industry as a whole offers less jobs than it did prior to the reunification. In the monthly report for December 2010 of the Federal Employment Agency we read: "There were still small losses in employment in the manufacturing sector."

The report supplies also the allegedly becalming explanation for this development: The restructuring towards the service sector is continuing in Germany. The share of the jobs subject to social insurance contributions in the service sector is increasing, while the share of the employees in the manufacturing sector decreases. According to the monthly report of the Federal Employment Agency (December 2011) in June, 2011, 69 per cent of the employees subject to social insurance contributions were working in a service industry (compared to 67.7 per cent in 2008) and 30.2 per cent in the manufacturing sector (compared to 31.5 per cent in 2008). Compared to the United States, Germany with 30 per cent of the working population in industry is better off than the U.S. where only some 11 per cent of the population still works in the manufacturing sector of the economy.

Moreover, following employment losses in the years 2009 and 2010 the number of employees in Germany's manufacturing sector (without construction) grew by 131,000 persons (1.7 per cent) in 2011 (Federal Bureau of Statistics press release, January 2, 2012).

No doubt: Offshoring is also a threat for Europe. The suction effect of the low wages in the emerging countries is too strong. The argument is naive that global competition will balance the incomes in the emerging countries and the industrial nations of the Western World. Even if the wages in, for example, China already are climbing, with hourly wages of less than 2 euro in emerging countries and fifteen times more in European countries, what would a balancing of wages look like? Where should wages balance? Wages would increase in the emerging countries and fall in the European countries. Unless prices in European countries fall with wages, the population will be facing significant income losses. These losses will be aggravated by the demographic development that is reducing the tax base for social insurance. Against this background, can we afford a balancing of wages on a world level?

From Crony Capitalism to Plutocracy

The prospects and ladders of upward mobility of the American middle class have been systematically destroyed by the deindustrialization of the country. From rags to riches—the American dream—is over. More and more citizens and families are falling from a comfortable middle class existence. Real incomes (adjusted for inflation) for most Americans are lower than they were years ago.[9]

There is little basis for economic improvement. American corporations have moved offshore millions of manufacturing and professional service jobs. For a consumer-driven economy, the loss of consumer incomes retards economic growth. The modest growth of the U.S. economy since the millennium was not real growth based on rising real income. It was an artificial growth created by artificially low interest rates and an expansion of consumer debt. When consumers reached the limit of the debt that they could service, the economy fell into recession.

Americans are not only losing their economy. They are losing their liberty. As far as domestic policy is concerned the face of the United States has undergone basic changes. Against the background of the war against the alleged terror threat important civil rights granted by the Constitution were abolished systematically within a few years. In his book, Paul Craig Roberts shows the degeneration of the U.S. into a warmongering police state.

To put it briefly, the America that Europeans knew during the second half of the 20th century does not exist any more. This is the most important epochal change to which we are contemporary witnesses. The European belief is that the Americans have always got back on their feet and will do so again, but this time might be different. The executive branch has freed itself of accountability to U.S. laws and to international law.

"In the course of human history every state sooner or later went broke or was conquered. Where do we get the arrogance to believe that our politicians are more intelligent than all their predecessors?" When Paul Craig Roberts at the occasion of a meeting in September 1993 in his office in Washington spoke those sentences he hardly expected that both could be true for his country not even 20 years later. Not only is the United States effectively bankrupt, but also the military-industrial complex and the financial oligarchy of the country have seized the power and initiated an unprecedented re-distribution of income, wealth, and power to the top. Super rich people are financing both large political parties, and with their unlimited financial means they decide on the results of both the presidential and the congressional elections.

Only recently, by ruling that this massive exertion of influence on election outcomes is merely the exercise of free speech, the U.S. Supreme Court gave its blessings to the private purchase of the U.S. government. Plutocratic power structures have developed out of the crony capitalism that now sets the agenda in Washington.

"There really are two Americas, one for the grifter class and one for everybody else," Matt Taibbi writes. "In everybody-else land the government would be something to be avoided. In the grifter world, however, government would be a slavish lapdog that the financial companies use as a tool for making money. The grifter class depends on these two positions getting confused in the minds of everybody else. They want the average American to believe that what government is to him, it is also to JP Morgan Chase and Goldman Sachs."[10]

How Much Longer Reserve Currency?

Apart from its military engagement in Arab states, America is fighting an economic war against the rest of the world – especially against Europe. At stake is the U.S. dollar's role as reserve currency and as anchor currency of the world financial system. It is a matter of financing the global power, the thirst for consumption, and the debt of the United States. With the U.S. dollar as anchor currency of the world, the United States has been in a very comfortable position since the middle of the 20th century: The U.S. can pay for its imports with its own currency. The U.S. does not have to earn foreign currencies by exporting in order to import. While the trade partners are delivering real goods like industrial products and crude oil, they receive fiat money in return, much of which is then converted into U.S. government bonds. For America's trade partners to finance the U.S. trade and budget deficits requires confidence that the U.S. dollar represents an adequate equivalent to the real goods and services. Considering the potentially disastrous economic situation of the United States today, this confidence is eroding.

The times have gone, in which the U.S. dollar was the unchallenged king of the currencies. Especially the euro has been a threat for the U.S. dollar. The same should increasingly apply to the yuan in the future. The Chinese government is working to establish the 'people's currency' (Renminbi) as an international trading currency. Only recently, it signed appropriate bilateral agreements with a number of countries. For example China and Japan agreed to directly trade their currencies since June 1, 2012. Moreover, the Chinese government strives to establish a yuan bond market and to achieve the free convertibility of the people's currency that was tied to the dollar. China can count on support from all over the world. Governments of other emerging countries have expressed the objective to end the global predominance of the U.S. dollar. They do not want to be at the mercy of U.S. financial policy.

In order to save its position, the U.S. government doesn't waste any opportunity to disguise the serious economic situation of its country. Roberts tells us to what extent the official statistics are being manipulated. On the other hand, in close cooperation with the Federal Reserve and the U.S. financial oligarchy, the U.S. government obviously wastes almost no opportunity to intervene against the euro in the global financial markets. The objective is clear: The weaker the euro appears, the surer and stronger the U.S. dollar appears, and the more likely investors are to buy U.S. Treasury debt and, thus, to finance the wars and budget deficit of the United States.

Quo Vadis Europe?

Against this background the developments in Europe are increasingly significant. The 'Old Continent' is also changing its face in these days. Which way will Europe finally take? The reply to this question determines the second epochal change to which we are contemporary witnesses.

This much seems clear: The European political elites are using the sovereign debt crisis to finally end the sovereignty of the European national states—especially also of Germany—and to bring the single countries of the eurozone under the control of a dirigiste bureaucratic central government. The goal is to establish the United States of Europe in the place of historically sovereign nations.

The founding fathers of the European unification envisioned the process of integration quite differently. They intended to build it upon a liberal regulatory policy that would establish and secure an anti-discriminatory competition between the member states. In paragraph 3 of the Treaty establishing the European Economic Community (EEC Treaty / Treaties of Rome) of 1957, it says: "For the purposes set out in Article 2, the activities of the Community shall include, as provided in this Treaty and in accordance with the timetable set out therein: the institution of a system ensuring that competition in the common market is not distorted.“

A good approach, because Europe distinguishes itself by its variety that grew over centuries. The continent consists of many and very different regions with unique cultural, culinary, linguistic, social, and political idiosyncrasies. Furthermore, there are very different mentalities and perceptions of life. Out of this variety Europe's strengths, Europe's creativity, and Europe's charm arose.

Instead of protecting these special idiosyncrasies with a liberal regulatory policy and to promote the competition between autonomous regions, the authorities in Bruxelles and Europe's political elites have been pursuing a dirigiste bureaucratic integration programme for roughly five decades that increasingly limits the scope for personal initiative, variety and the richness of human mind in society, state and economy. The centralistic orientated Bruxelles is steadily expanding its power and sphere of influence. "The markets and other areas of life shall be 'gripped' with planning methods in order to subordinate the 'mircrostructural' substructure of the economy to superior 'macrostructural' objectives—by guidelines on technical and economical efficiency standards, by criteria for best sites, by minimum wages and other 'social standards', by regulating currency-exchange, by standardized interest rates, tax rates, and aid rates, by structural funds, regional funds, and cohesion funds, by an European financial compensation and forms of collective responsibility for sovereign debt," summaries Prof. Dr. Alfred Schüller (the tools of the one size-fits-all policy in the ORDO[11] yearbook). Bureaucrats in Bruxelles are seizing responsibility for judging and deciding what should be the measure of all things for the different European nationalities. Entire Europe is about to be levelled and "normalized." Even fruits and vegetables should orient themselves on standards cogitated by highly paid bureaucrats in Bruxelles.[12]

It is foreseeable: European variety will be the casualty. Laws, rules of action, and other guidelines predetermined by Bruxelles will increasingly limit the scopes of the citizens. They establish obstacles and disincentives to entrepreneurial behavior. In doing so the centralistic oriented Bruxelles is destroying livelihoods on a large scale. It can only weaken the economic power of the continent.

Only Europe's bureaucracy and political elites will be the beneficiaries of the 'United States of Europe' including a central government in Bruxelles. To err is human. Governments make mistakes. The more power they have and the more far-reaching their decisions are, the more far-reaching are the consequences of their mistakes. Prof. Dr. Erich Weede, professor emeritus of the University of Bonn, points out this aspect. The entire European continent has to suffer from mistakes the central power in Bruxelles makes. For this reason we should resist any further centralization of power in Bruxelles. There is a great danger that the centralized power in Bruxelles will develop the same way as the central government in Washington and that Europe also degenerates into a plutocracy.

Already in 1970s with the "Snake in the tunnel" and the "European Monetary System" (EMS) some European states tried to coordinate their currencies and monetary policy. Already at that time the currency-exchange rates could not be stabilized within the exchange rate mechanism in the desired way. The economic performance of the countries and their political orientation were too different. The failure of these experiments was not surprising. It would have been enough to take a look into history. "Seen from a historical perspective, politically stabilized currency-exchange rates have rarely been of long lasting nature," writes Werner Plumpe, professor of economic and social history at the Goethe University of Frankfurt am Main.[13]

Nevertheless, Europe's political elites decided to introduce the common currency euro as book money on January 1, 1999, and as cash money on January 1, 2002 – from today's perspective the first decisive step on the way towards a centralized European central state. The majority of Germans, who would have preferred to keep the D-Mark, were sceptical. They were afraid the common currency would not be as stable as the D-Mark, although the D-Mark since its introduction in 1948 already had lost some 90 per cent of its purchasing power. On February 7, 1992, the "Treaty on European Union" (Maastricht Treaty) was signed into law. It determined the "convergence criteria" (Maastricht criteria)[14] that were bound to commit all members of the eurozone to a track of stability. However, no mechanism was created to sanction violations of the agreements without any ifs and buts. The wool was pulled over the eyes of the citizens.

"Maximum limits both for the annually new indebtedness and the debt level of public households have been agreed on. Should they be exceeded the union mandatorily can recommend reductions and, under circumstances, enforce them with fines. This ensures a sound fiscal policy also after the entry into the currency union." So they said in the brochure, "The euro – as strong as the mark," which was published by the Federal Ministry of Finance in April 1996. "Also after the onset of the currency union care is taken to ensure that no member will leave the path of virtue and stability." Today, many paragraphs of this brochure sound like derision: "Regarding the convergence criteria the treaty must be strictly observed; a maceration will not occur."

The contract was breached—also by the German red-green federal government. Likewise, the purchase of government bonds by the European Central Bank (ECB) in the spring of 2010 was clearly a breach of law. In this context, one notion George Soros expressed in the Financial Times on Juliy 13, 2011, is interesting. The architects of the euro "laboured under the misconception that financial markets can correct their own excesses, so the rules were designed to rein in only public-sector excesses. Even there, they relied too heavily on self-policing by sovereign states."

The End of the European National States

With the Stability Pact the eurozone takes the second decisive step towards a centralized European unity state. Again, the future of the European economy builds on promises. Like the federal government of Helmut Kohl, the government of Angela Merkel counts on an obviously illusory hope that the stability policy about which the heads of the governments agreed will prevail in the countries of the eurozone in the long run. But this time the European establishment goes the whole hog: With the "European Stability Mechanism" (ESM) the countries of the eurozone shall irrevocably abandon a great deal of their fiscal sovereignty to Bruxelles. "The ESM Treaty is a mockery and derision as far as sanity and reason but also as far as European juridical traditions are concerned. With this ESM Treaty, a small group of governments revolt against their own people," says Rolf von Hohenhau, president of the Taxpayers Association of Europe.[15]

"The Greek economic infrastructure in no way is comparable with ours, and the interlacing of the Greek foreign trade with trade flows in the eurozone is very narrow." No, this is not a quote by a euro castigator but by

Eurogroup chaiman Jean-Claude Juncker. And he said this at the end of February 2012.[16] Are the economic infrastructures of the other European countries comparable with each other? Why do we have to try to make them comparable by hook or by crook or by force?

Additionally, Juncker claims to appoint a "EU commissioner charged with the task of building up the structure of the Greek economy" and to "think and think ahead" Greece's economic policy. In other words, a bureaucrat from Bruxelles shall replace the individual and entrepreneurial initiatives of the Greeks. What will happen to the other countries of Southern Europe should their citizens vote out the "stability policy" of their current governments in future elections? Will EU commissioners take over the economic policy of all those countries? Even against the citizens will? Former ECB president Jean-Claude Trichet makes no secret of his thoughts: In extreme cases the EU countries shall declare countries bankrupt and take over their fiscal policy.

No doubt where the journey goes. Among others, José Manuel Barroso as president of the EU commission, France's new president Francois Hollande, Italy's prime minister Mario Monti or monetary affairs commissioner Olli Rehn call for merging the debts of the separate governments of the eurozone through Eurobonds. In the eyes of France's new prime minister, Jean-Marc Ayrault, the ECB shall finance the crisis-hit countries directly, thus to unite Europe's finance in one policy.

A paradigm shift is taking place. The self-responsibility—the sovereignty—of the European countries is being abolished step by step. "European countries will become like once independent American states, subservient to central power that rules from afar," Paul Craig Roberts writes. Key representatives of this central power are not elected directly by the peoples of the EU. For example the president of the EU commision is nominated by the European Council and is elected by the European Parliament for five years.

In particular, for Germany the scheme is likely to backfire: The German economic policy will be increasingly determined through Bruxelles and determined more and more by the fiscally more clueless mentality of the southern countries. As by far the strongest economic power of Europe Germany will have to pay for an experiment that is condemned to failure.

Right from the beginning, the euro was a political currency[17] lacking an economic base. A number of economists had warned: Given such a different performance of the economies of the participating countries, a common currency can't possibly work. Their warnings remained unheard.

Obviously, the political elites do not want to acknowledge the destructive power that resides inside the euro. Even proponents of the euro are inadvertently delivering arguments against the common currency. According to the study, "The Future of the Euro," compiled by McKinsey Germany, the euro accelerates the destruction of labor-intensive industries such as shipbuilding that traditionally are located in the peripheral countries of the eurozone. "The euro introduced a hard currency to all countries and emphasised the need for wage restraints to restore competitiveness in these industries. Consequently, the euro caused an imminent need for structural change towards new industries that are less focused on cost to avoid price competition with emerging low-cost countries."[18] What industries can these be in the age of globalism and the increasing competitive pressure from emerging countries?

Despite its structural deficits since its introduction, the euro as an alternative to the U.S. dollar gained ground in the global monetary policy. In the year 2006 the common currency replaced the U.S. Dollar as the worldwide leading cash money—although one reason for this is the fact that in the United States less and less purchases are paid for with cash. Also, the euro's share of the global currency reserves already is above 25 per cent.

The advocates of the euro invoke the removal of currency risks in trade between the countries of the eurozone, the removal of fees on money exchange, the alleged higher economic growth in the eurozone, and the alleged peacemaking impact as the major advantages of the common currency. They disregard what might be the most important point: Against the background of the precarious economic situation of the United States the euro had the potential to replace the Greenback as reserve currency of the world. In this case, Europe would really benefit from the Euro since the Old Continent would be in the comfortable position to pay for its imports and debt with money it prints on its own (like the U.S.). So the euro could indeed create wealth by creating fiat money.

But the European political establishment proved to be unable to build the integration process on a liberal regulatory policy and sound fiscal policy. For this reason the euro suffers from questions about its future viability. The U.S. financial oligarchy and U.S. government authorities have incentives to act against the euro on the global financial markets, because the euro's problems distract attention from the real situation of the U.S. dollar.

Keep in mind that U.S. financial institutions sold many toxic assets to European banks in the course of the U.S. real estate bubble. Since the bubble burst major European banks have been facing the threat of insolvency. By deciding to bail out the European banks from Wall Street's toxic waste, European governments created the precedent for bailing out the banks from their over-lending to sovereign governments.

Paul Craig Roberts observes that Washington prefers a centralized United States of Europe. Compared to Europe's variety of independent national governments, a few of which might occasionally produce real leadership, it is easier for the White House to control a central government in Brussels. One of the reasons that Washington is provoking the Russian government is to make Europeans fearful of Russian response and more compliant to Washington's wishes.

The future of the euro is open. Paul Craig Roberts recommends that Germany resign from the eurozone. Instead of tying itself to the ragged European neighbour countries and risking Germany's exploitation in a transfer union, Germany with its economic power would do better to orientate itself towards the emerging economic powers and enter a cooperation especially with Russia, a country rich in natural resources. Such cooperation would automatically create a suction effect and would rope in at least the Eastern European countries. In this cooperation the national governments would keep their economic sovereignty and abdicate a common currency.

Critique of the Growth Model

Paul Craig Roberts sold supply-side economics to the U.S. Congress and to President Reagan as the way to overcome stagflation (simultaneously rising inflation and unemployment) and renew economic growth. Why does he now write that growth might be the problem instead of the solution? "I dealt with the problems of my time. Supply-side economics worked, and the worsening trade-offs between inflation and unemployment disappeared for two decades. Today's problems are different, and they are dealt with in this book."

On the one hand there are theoretical problems in the growth model. On the other hand the growth model is not being applied in Europe to what is euphemistically called "the sovereign debt problem," but in reality is the problem of reckless lending by private banks. Austerity is being imposed in order to free resources with which to pay the banks, and the austerity is driving growth into the ground. In other words, the West itself does not believe that its growth model is the solution to the problem.

Another problem is that the growth model no longer works for many people. For example, in the U.S. income growth is only experienced by a small percentage at the top. In much of the Third World the growth model imposes monocultures that deprive people of independence and self-sufficiency. Yet another problem is that the growth model is not sustainable as it is exhausting nature's capital and is polluting our planet. When one thinks about such things as the economists' assumption that man-made capital is a substitute for nature's capital, one realizes that this unrealistic assumption (known as the Solow-Stiglitz production function) is the basis of the belief that economic growth is infinitely sustainable. Growth cannot be infinite when earth's resources are finite. "Therefore," writes Roberts, "we must think anew prior to the exhaustion of nature's capital. Long-run thinking must supplant short-term thinking."

Many industrial, agricultural, and food-producing processes pollute air, water, and soil. Corporations avoid costs by imposing them on the environment. In some instances these external costs exceed the value of the corporations' output. The quality of food, its nutrition and safety are sacrificed for yield.

The exhaustion of nature's capital has begun to bite. Surface water and aquifers are threatened by fracking, mining, and chemical fertilizer run-off. Even some pastures have become deadly to cattle. Many cities have many days during which air pollution is a health threat. The notion that the entire world can live at a 20th century American consumption level seems farfetched and unattainable. Yet, it remains the goal of the world's policymakers. Drawing on the work of others, such as former World Bank economist Herman Daly, Roberts suggests that a "steady state" economy that provides adequate material means for material life and preservation of nature's capital, not mass consumption societies, is the only sustainable economic model.

Clearly, this empirically based, theoretically challenging book is one of the most important works of our time.

INTRODUCTION

The collapse of the Soviet Union in 1991 and the rise of the high speed Internet have proved to be the economic and political undoing of the West. "The End of History" caused socialist India and communist China to join the winning side and to open their economies and underutilized labor forces to Western capital and technology. Pushed by Wall Street and large retailers such as Wal-Mart, American corporations began offshoring the production of goods and services for their domestic markets. Americans ceased to be employed in the manufacture of goods that they consume as corporate executives maximized shareholder earnings and their performance bonuses by substituting cheaper foreign labor for American labor. Many American professional occupations, such as software engineering and Information Technology, also declined as corporations moved this work abroad and brought in foreigners at lower remuneration for many of the jobs that remained domestically. Design and research jobs followed manufacturing abroad, and employment in middle class professional occupations ceased to grow. By taking the lead in offshoring production for domestic markets, US corporations force the same practice on Europe. The demise of First World employment and of Third World agricultural communities, which are supplanted by large scale monoculture, is known as Globalism.

For most Americans income has stagnated and declined for the past two decades. Much of what Americans lost in wages and salaries as their jobs were moved offshore came back to shareholders and executives in the form of capital gains and performance bonuses from the higher profits that flowed from lower foreign labor costs. The distribution of income worsened dramatically with the mega-rich capturing the gains, while the middle class ladders of upward mobility were dismantled. University graduates unable to find employment returned to live with their parents.

The absence of growth in real consumer incomes resulted in the Federal Reserve expanding credit in order to keep consumer demand growing. The growth of consumer debt was substituted for the missing growth in consumer income. The Federal Reserve's policy of extremely low interest rates fueled a real estate boom. Housing prices rose dramatically, permitting homeowners to monetize the rising equity in their homes by refinancing their mortgages.

Consumers kept the economy alive by assuming larger mortgages and spending the equity in their homes and by accumulating large credit card balances. The explosion of debt was securitized, given fraudulent investment grade ratings, and sold to unsuspecting investors at home and abroad.

Financial deregulation, which began in the Clinton years and leaped forward during the George W. Bush regime, unleashed greed and debt leverage. Brooksley Born, head of the federal Commodity Futures Trading Commission, was prevented from regulating over-the-counter derivatives by the chairman of the Federal Reserve, the Secretary of the Treasury, and the chairman of the Securities and Exchange Commission. The financial stability of the world was sacrificed to the ideology of these three stooges that "markets are self-regulating." Insurance companies sold credit default swaps against junk financial instruments without establishing reserves, and financial institutions leveraged every dollar of equity with $30 dollars of debt.

When the bubble burst, the former bankers running the US Treasury provided massive bailouts at taxpayer expense for the irresponsible gambles made by banks that they formerly headed. The Federal Reserve joined the rescue operation. An audit of the Federal Reserve released in July, 2011 revealed that the Federal Reserve had provided $16 trillion—a sum larger than US GDP or the US public debt—in secret loans to bail out American and foreign banks, while doing nothing to aid the millions of American families being foreclosed out of their homes. Political accountability disappeared as all public assistance was directed to the mega-rich, whose greed had produced the financial crisis.

The financial crisis and plight of the banksters took center stage and prevented recognition that the crisis sprang not only from the financial deregulation but also from the expansion of debt that was used to substitute for the lack of growth in consumer income. As more and more jobs were offshored, Americans were deprived of incomes from employment. To maintain their consumption, Americans went deeper into debt.

The fact that millions of jobs have been moved offshore is the reason why the most expansionary monetary and fiscal policies in US history have had no success in reducing the unemployment rate.

The reason the unemployment rate is dropping is that Americans unable to find jobs are dropping out of the labor force and are no longer counted as unemployed. In the post-World War II 20th century recessions, laid-off workers were called back to work as expansionary monetary and fiscal policies stimulated consumer demand. However, 21st century unemployment is different. The jobs have been moved abroad and no longer exist. Therefore, workers cannot be called back to factories and to professional service jobs that have been moved abroad."

Economists have failed to recognize the threat that jobs off-shoring poses to economies and to economic theory itself, because economists confuse offshoring with free trade, which they believe is mutually beneficial. I will show that offshoring is the antithesis of free trade and that the doctrine of free trade itself is found to be incorrect by the latest work in trade theory. Indeed, as we reach toward a new economics, cherished assumptions and comforting theoretical conclusions will be shown to be erroneous.

This book is organized into three sections. The first section explains successes and failures of economic theory and the erosion of the efficacy of economic policy by globalism. Globalism and financial concentration have destroyed the justifications of market capitalism. Corporations that have become "too big to fail" are sustained by public subsidies, thus destroying capitalism's claim to be an efficient allocator of resources. Profits no longer are a measure of social welfare when they are obtained by creating unemployment and declining living standards in the home country.

The second section documents how jobs offshoring or globalism and financial deregulation wrecked the US economy, producing high rates of unemployment, poverty and a distribution of income and wealth extremely skewed toward a tiny minority at the top. These severe problems cannot be corrected within a system of globalism.

The third section addresses the European debt crisis and how it is being used both to subvert national sovereignty and to protect bankers from losses by imposing austerity and bailout costs on citizens of the member countries of the European Union.

I will suggest that it is in Germany's interest to leave the EU, revive the mark, and enter into an economic partnership with Russia. German industry, technology, and economic and financial rectitude, combined with Russian energy and raw materials, would pull all of Eastern Europe into a new economic union, with each country retaining its own currency and budgetary and tax authority. This would break up NATO, which has become an instrument for world oppression and is forcing Europeans to assume the burdens of the American Empire.

Sixty-eight years after the end of World War II, twenty-three years after the reunification of Germany, and twenty-two years after the collapse of the Soviet Union, Germany is still occupied by US troops. Do Europeans desire a future as puppet states of a collapsing empire, or do they desire a more promising future of their own?

PART I

PROBLEMS IN ECONOMIC THEORY

From the Anglo-American perspective, economic theory originated with Adam Smith in the 18th century. In the early 19th century, Britisher David Ricardo made the case for free trade based on comparative advantage. Another Britisher, Alfred Marshall, explained the formation of prices in the late 19th century, and yet another Britisher, John Maynard Keynes, gave us macroeconomics in the third decade of the 20th century. A couple of decades later, an American economist, Milton Friedman, gave us monetarism. Of course, Germans, Austrians, Italians and Frenchmen made contributions, but Smith-Ricardo-Marshall-Keynes-Friedman provided the economic corpus, encompassing free trade, price formation, and the stability of prices and employment.

In the post-war 20th century the economics that most affected the public was macroeconomics. Unemployment and inflation were the two rival problems.

What follows is a brief account of how post-war economics, initially successful, fell into problems from its neglect of the supply-side of the economy and from an uncritical acceptance of a country's transfer of its capital, technology, and jobs to another country. This transfer continues to be misinterpreted as the mutually beneficial workings of free trade. In fact the transfer is the result of the pursuit of absolute advantage—the antithesis of free trade.

Microeconomics

Economics can successfully explain the efficient allocation of resources by the price system and the allocation of investment by profitability. Relatively speaking, these successes are new. It was Alfred Marshall at the end of the 19th century who explained price formation. Prior to Marshall, economists debated whether price was determined by the cost of production or by demand—what people were willing to pay. Marshall ended the controversy by pointing out that supply and demand are the two blades of the scissors. Together they determine price.

Profit is the return on capital. A normal profit depends on time and circumstances. It is the profit necessary to retain capital in an activity. If capital cannot earn a normal rate of return in an activity, capital is not supplied to that activity. This ensures that capital is not wasted in low value uses. Whenever capital earns a higher than normal return, it is a sign that it is employed in a high value use. The excess profits will lead to an expansion of investment in that use until profits are reduced to normal.

Without price and profit signals, there is no way of knowing how to efficiently use resources to produce the highest valued output. The Soviet economy failed because the system's gross output indicators, the main signal of managerial and plan success, could not tell if outputs were more valuable than inputs.

The study of the price system is known as micro-economics. It is the soundest field of economics. "Free prices" simply means the freedom of prices to change with supply and demand. It does not mean laissez faire or no rules and regulations. The "free market" means the freedom of prices to change as conditions change.

Macroeconomics

Economists concluded from the Great Depression that a price system could function without ensuring full employment. This conclusion led to the rise of macroeconomics, the study of the factors leading to the overall level of prices and employment.

With his 1936 book, *The General Theory of Employment, Interest and Money*, John Maynard Keynes established himself as the First macroeconomist. His book resulted in Keynesian economics, of which the American economist Paul Samuelson was doyen. Keynesian macroeconomists concluded that employment and the price level depend on the level of total spending. If consumers saved more than investors invested, the result would be a leakage from the spending stream and a shortage of aggregate demand (the total demand for resources from consumption and investment). The shortfall in spending would cause a decline in employment and prices.

On the other hand, if there were an excess of spending, the demand on resources would drive up prices and the economy would experience inflation.

Macroeconomists concluded that the way to manage the economy was for the government to manage demand. If there was insufficient spending to maintain full employment, the government would fill in the gap by running a deficit in its budget. That is, the government would spend more than it received in tax revenues, thus adding to aggregate demand (consumption + investment + government).

If there was too much spending, the government would reduce the amount by running a budget surplus. In other words, the government would collect more in tax revenues than it would spend, thus contracting the spending stream.

The Keynesians grasped the importance of aggregate demand, but the only economist (a physical chemist actually) who got it right was Michael Polanyi in his 1945 book, *Full Employment and Free Trade* (Cambridge University Press). Polanyi anticipated Milton Friedman and the American monetarists. Polanyi interpreted Keynes' theory to mean that widespread unemployment meant that there was *a dearth of money*. What the government needed to do was to expand the monetary circulation. It could do this, Polanyi noted, simply by printing money to finance its deficit.

Polanyi made more important deductions than the Keynesians. He said that it was expensive for the government to borrow money, on which it had to pay interest, in order to cover its deficit and that this expense was pointless. Government could more cheaply provide the missing purchasing power by printing the money to cover its budget deficit. In other words, Polanyi understood Keynes to mean that fiscal policy is a way to expand the money supply when reluctance or impaired ability to borrow and lend prevented the central bank from expanding the supply of money.

In 1945, Polanyi's conclusions were too advanced for the economics profession. But two decades later, in the 1960s, Milton Friedman and Anna Schwartz made it clear that the Great Depression in the U.S. during the 1930s was caused by Federal Reserve mistakes that resulted in one-third shrinkage in the supply of money. The depression in the UK following World War I resulted from the decision by the British government to go back on the gold standard at the prewar parity of the British pound sterling and gold. As the British money supply had expanded so much, the return to gold at prewar parity required shrinkage in the money supply, a shrinkage that collapsed employment and prices in the UK.

Thus, the Keynesians, who had the right idea, initially did not understand that full employment is a monetary phenomenon. If government spends more by borrowing to finance its deficit, its borrowing reduces spending on consumption and investment in the same way as taxation does. A budget deficit can boost consumer demand only if the central bank accommodates the deficit by expanding the money supply.

The Keynesians' second mistake came from their failure to understand the impact of fiscal policy on supply. To maintain full employment, the Keynesians came to rely on monetary expansion. Keynesian demand management kept money and credit abundant to ensure sufficient spending. To restrain inflation, Keynesians relied on high tax rates to withdraw spending power from the population that the easy monetary policy provided. The Keynesian economists believed that high taxes served to reduce consumer demand to noninflationary levels. In fact, high tax rates reduced the supply of labor and the supply of goods and services, while easy money pushed up consumer demand. Consequently, prices rose.

The Keynesian demand management policy came unglued and failed during the Carter administration in the late 1970s. Worsening trade-offs between inflation and unemployment left macroeconomists with no policy solution except wage and price controls. In other words, the failure of macroeconomics meant that the price system would not be allowed to allocate resources. Unable to remedy the cause of inflation, Keynesians proposed using government coercion to prevent wages and prices from rising.

Congress was unhappy with this proposal. Congress had recently had an experience with fixing one price—the price of oil—and it had been a disaster. Congress was in no mood to fix all prices. Congress preferred to listen to new voices, the voices of "supply-side economists" (in contrast to Keynesian "demand-side economists"). Supply-side economists were new macroeconomists who had a policy with both blades of the scissors. They pointed out that in Keynesian macroeconomics, fiscal policy (changes in tax rates or changes in government spending) only affects aggregate demand: higher taxes reduce consumer purchasing power and aggregate demand declines; lower taxes increase consumer purchasing power and aggregate demand rises. Supply-side economists said that, in fact, changes in marginal tax rates (the rate of tax on additions to income) *change aggregate supply.*

Supply-side economics is a correction to Keynesian demand management. It has nothing to do with "trickle-down economics" or with a claim that tax cuts pay for themselves. Supply-side economics says that some fiscal policies shift the aggregate supply curve, not the aggregate demand curve. Specifically, if marginal tax rates are raised, aggregate supply will decline. There will be fewer goods and services supplied at every price. If marginal tax rates are lowered, aggregate supply will increase; there will be more goods and services available at every price.

Today, this conclusion is no longer controversial, but in the 1970s it was a new thought. Initially, Keynesians resisted it, but Paul Samuelson came to terms with supply-side economics in the twelfth edition of his economics textbook and accepted in principle the relative price effects of fiscal policy.

By bringing relative prices that affect individual behavior into macroeconomics, supply-side economists integrated microeconomics with macroeconomics, a long-standing goal that economics had not achieved. Supply-side economists showed that a shift in marginal tax rates changes relative prices and affects individual decisions whether to save more or to consume more, and whether to work more or to enjoy more leisure. The allocation of income between saving (investment) and consumption and the allocation of time between work and leisure affect the growth rate of the economy.[1]

Think about it this way. The cost of current consumption is the foregone future income from saving and investment. Income is an after-tax phenomenon. The higher the tax rate on income, the less current consumption costs in terms of foregone future income or, in other words, the less future income is given up by today's consumption. The lower the tax rate, the larger the amount of future income that is lost by consuming instead of investing.

For example, consider the 98 percent tax rate on investment income that was the rule in England prior to Prime Minister Margaret Thatcher. Suppose a person has 100,000 pounds. Shall he invest it or purchase a Rolls Royce? If he invests the money at, say, 10 percent, he would earn 10,000 pounds before tax. But after-tax, his earnings would be reduced to 200 pounds. Thus, the opportunity cost of the Rolls Royce is only 200 pounds a year in foregone income. The high tax rate on investment income makes current consumption extremely inexpensive in terms of foregone income.

If the tax rate on investment income is 15 percent, the cost of the Rolls Royce in terms of foregone income would be 8,500 pounds per year, or 42.5 times as much annually. The 98 percent tax rate on investment income makes the Rolls Royce essentially a free good. The 15 percent tax rate makes the car purchase expensive.

Similarly, the cost of leisure is the income given up by not working. The higher the tax rate, the less the after-tax income lost by using time for leisure instead of work. The lower the tax rate, the more expensive is leisure in terms of foregone income. The marginal tax rate on earned income thus affects the supply of labor.

Supply-side economics also corrected a mistake in capital theory. Economists taught that the interest rate determines the cost of capital. If the interest rate is high, capital is costly and investment small. If the interest rate is low, capital is cheap and investment flourishes. At one time this theory made sense, and that time was prior to the income tax. Capital theory originated prior to the income tax, and until supply-side economists came along, no adjustment had been made for the impact of taxation on the cost of capital. When there is an income tax, profits or the earnings of capital are an after-tax phenomenon. The higher the tax rates, the higher the cost of capital, and the lower is investment and the growth of the economy.[2]

Supply-side economists added supply to the macroeconomic scissors. Prior to supply-side economics in the 1970s, macroeconomics was stuck in the pre-Marshallian past. The stagflation that destroyed Jimmy Carter's presidency was induced by policy. Demand-side Keynesians pumped up consumer demand with easy money, while they restrained output with high tax rates. The result was stagflation.

People unfamiliar with facts claim that it was Federal Reserve chairman Paul Volcker's tight monetary policy that cured stagflation. This erroneous claim ignores that prior to the Reagan administration's supply-side policy, tight monetary policy had had no effect on stagflation. Indeed, all Volcker's tight money did was to drive interest rates on money market funds to 17 per cent, thus providing plenty of consumer spending power to drive inflation higher while high tax rates suppressed investment. A person with

$100,000 in savings in a money market fund was receiving $17,000 a year in pre-tax income.

Today, Keynesian economics has been reconciled with monetarism and with supply-side economics, making macroeconomics a coherent whole.

However, today macroeconomic policy faces new challenges. In the 21st century, the U.S. economy has been kept going by an expansion in consumer debt, not by rises in consumers' real incomes. Burdened with large credit card and mortgage debt, consumers are no longer in a position to borrow more in order to spend more. Interest rates are very low, and the government's budget deficit is very large; yet, high unemployment persists.

Monetary and fiscal policy cannot help when the problem is that American jobs have been relocated offshore. Because of offshore production, stimulating demand stimulates production in China and other offshore sites. As high-productivity jobs have been offshored, American incomes, except for those of the super-rich, have ceased to grow. Thus, there is no effective way to boost consumer spending short of printing money and giving it to the population, or handing out tax rebates accommodated by monetary expansion.

Prior to the collapse of world socialism and the rise of the high-speed Internet, it was not possible to offshore jobs or production for U.S. markets to any significant extent. In those prior times, American incomes rose with productivity. If a glitch in employment occurred, an expansionary demand-side or supply-side policy would boost employment and GDP. Today, the jobs have been moved abroad. The jobs are not waiting on an expansionary policy to call Americans back to work.

Trade deficits mean that consumers have spent their money on goods produced abroad at the expense of domestic

GDP and employment growth. Writing on the *CounterPunch* website (Dec. 11, 2008), economist Peter Morici reports that U.S. GDP is $1.5 trillion smaller as a result of the record trade deficits accumulated over the previous 10 years.

$1.5 trillion is still a large sum. Without this loss in GDP, there would be $5,000 in additional income for each one of the 300,000,000 Americans. A family of four would have $20,000 additional income.

A country that gives away its productive capability and GDP and becomes dependent on foreign creditors to finance its budget and trade deficits is a country that has problems beyond the reach of monetary and fiscal policies. For example, no country's borrowing ability is unlimited. The U.S. has been financing its trade and budget deficits by turning over the ownership of existing U.S. assets and their income streams to foreigners and by foreigners recycling their trade surplus dollars into the purchase of new U.S. Treasury debt. This dependence on foreign creditors constrains U.S. monetary and fiscal policy.

Such creditors hold most of their reserves in dollar-denominated assets. The low interest rates and large budget deficits that are the traditional macroeconomic response to recession make America's creditors reluctant to add to their dollar holdings. The question has risen whether the U.S. can continue to hemorrhage debt and retain its reserve currency role. If the U.S. dollar is dethroned as reserve currency, the U.S. would no longer be able to pay its bills in its own currency. Such a development would complicate America's financing needs. The U.S. has become an import-dependent country, dependent on foreigners for energy, manufactured goods, and advanced technology products.

The U.S. has been able to consume more than it produces and to borrow more than it saves because the dollar is the reserve currency. Other countries that get into such a situation either go broke and lose all access to credit or accept an International Monetary Fund austerity program that forces them to curtail consumption and to pay down debt. For the U.S., an IMF austerity program would mean a substantial reduction in living standards.

What can be done? As it would be very difficult for the U.S. to get its house in order if it were to lose the reserve currency role, the government should take immediate action to preserve this role. Preserving the dollar as reserve currency requires large reductions in trade and budget deficits, a tall order for the current weak state of the U.S. economy.

The U.S. could reduce the budget deficit by hundreds of billions of dollars by ending its pointless and illegal wars, by closing hundreds of overseas military bases, and by cutting an overstuffed military budget. This would require the U.S. to give up its goal of world hegemony, but now that America's creditors have seen its aggressiveness, and this aggressiveness shows signs of turning toward China and Russia, creditors are unlikely to continue financing U.S. militarism. In the absence of foreign financing of U.S. deficits, or of insufficient foreign savings to cover annual U.S. budget deficits in excess of one trillion dollars, the Federal Reserve would have to monetize the U.S. deficit by purchasing the bond issues. Large scale debt monetization can result in high rates of inflation.

Unfortunately, debt monetization is what the Federal Reserve chose with its policy of Quantitative Easing. For several years the Federal Reserve has been purchasing $1,000 billion of bonds per year in order to finance the federal budget deficit and keep the prices of debt-related derivatives high on the insolvent banks' books. So far this newly created money has been trapped within the banking system and has not entered into the economy, where the inflow of dollars would push up prices. Instead, Quantitative Easing has put pressure on the exchange value of the US dollar. To protect the dollar from Quantitative Easing, Washington has prevailed on other countries to inflate their own currencies so that the dollar is not the only currency being printed. As I have pointed out in articles on my website, www.paulcraigroberts.org, the Federal Reserve has also been rigging the bullion market by selling naked shorts in order to drive down the prices of gold and silver, thus making the dollar appear to be the only safe refuge.

In traditional economic analysis, rising domestic unemployment curtails imports as consumers have less income to spend, thus reducing the trade deficit. The U.S. needs to do much more. U.S. manufacturing has declined so much that, should its creditors permit, the time is not far off when the U.S. trade deficit becomes as large a share of GDP as its manufacturing output.

Offshored production needs to be brought home. When corporations offshore their production for U.S. markets, they reduce U.S. GDP and increase the trade deficit, dollar for dollar.

The U.S. could bring home its offshored production by abolishing the corporate income tax and taxing corporations according to whether value is added to their products at home or abroad. Corporations that produce their products in the U.S. would have a low rate of tax; those that offshore their production would have a high rate of tax.

This change would take time to become effective, and in the near term it could anger creditors, such as China, a country where production for the U.S. market has raised employment and income. However, if the policy of bringing production home was seen as credible, the world would see a renewed prospect for the U.S. dollar as reserve currency.

Another helpful reform would be to overthrow performance pay for management based on short-term profits. Quarterly reporting and the cap on executive pay that is not performance based gives U.S. corporate executives a very short-time horizon compared to overseas competitors.

These suggestions would have to overcome powerful vested interests. Moreover, the hubris of American elites might outlast the window of opportunity that exists for the renewal of the U.S. economy.

Free Trade Error

Until recently, economists believed that the case for free trade was unassailable. Most economists still think that the case is secure. However, the two necessary conditions for David Ricardo's 200-year-old theory are no longer present in the modern world. Moreover, the latest work in trade theory, *Global Trade and Conflicting National Interests* (MIT Press, 2000), by Ralph E. Gomory and William J. Baumol, shows that the case for free trade was incorrect from the beginning.

Let's begin with the original case for free trade. It is based on the principle of comparative advantage. This principle says that it pays for countries to specialize and to trade even if one country can produce all tradable goods at a lower cost than the other country. This conclusion follows from countries having different "opportunity costs" of producing tradable goods. The opportunity cost of any good is the other goods that could have been produced by the same resources.

Ricardo uses as examples wine and wool. Portugal can produce both wine and wool cheaper than England, but Portugal has to give up more bottles of wine to gain a yard of woolen cloth than England. Thus, Portugal has a comparative advantage in producing wine, and England has a comparative advantage in producing wool. If each country specializes where it has comparative advantage, the total production of wine and wool will be greater than if each country produced both products. "The gains from trade" result from sharing the increase in total output by trading the two commodities on terms favorable to both countries. Therefore, specialization and trade will allow each country more consumption of both products than if each country were self-sufficient.

The different opportunity costs of one good in terms of another (the cost of wine in terms of wool) means that the trading partners have different relative price ratios for producing tradable goods. It is this difference that creates comparative advantage. In Ricardo's time, unique national characteristics, climate, and geography were important determinants of relative costs. Today, however, most combinations of inputs that produce outputs are knowledge-based. The relative price ratios are the same in every country. Therefore, as opportunity costs do not differ across national boundaries, there is no basis for comparative advantage.

Ricardo's other necessary condition for comparative advantage is that a country's capital seeks its comparative advantage in its home country and does not seek more productive use abroad. Ricardo confronts the possibility that English capital might migrate to Portugal to take advantage of the lower costs of production, thus leaving the English workforce unemployed, or employed in less productive ways. He is able to dismiss this undermining of comparative advantage because of "the difficulty with which capital moves from one country to another" and because capital is insecure "when not under the immediate control of its owner." This insecurity, "fancied or real," together "with the natural disinclination which every man has to quit the country of his birth and connections, and entrust himself, with all his habits fixed, to a strange government and new laws, check the emigration of capital. These feelings, which

I should be sorry to see weakened, induce most men of property to be satisfied with a low rate of profits in their own country, rather than seek a more advantageous employment for their wealth in foreign lands."

Today, these feelings have been weakened. Men of property have been replaced by corporations. Once the large excess supplies of Asian labor were available to American corporations, once Congress limited the tax deductibility of CEO pay that was not "performance related," once Wall Street pressured corporations for higher shareholder returns, once Wal-Mart ordered its suppliers to meet "the Chinese price," once hostile takeovers could be justified as improving shareholder returns by offshoring production, capital and jobs departed the country.

Capital has become as mobile as traded goods. Indeed, capital can move with the speed of light, but traded goods have to move by ship or airplane. Economists would be hard-pressed to produce stories of American capital seeking comparative advantage in the 50 states. But they can easily show its flight abroad. Approximately half of U.S. imports from China are the offshored production of U.S. firms for the U.S. market.

Most economists, whom I have labeled "no-think economists," learned in graduate school that to question free trade was to be a protectionist—a designation that could harm one's career. I personally know many economists who are terrified to be anything but free traders, but who have no understanding of the theory on which free trade is based or of the theory's many problems.

For most economists, free trade is a dictum like the Bush regime's dictum that Saddam Hussein had "weapons of mass destruction." The eight year, three trillion dollar war was pointless, just as is the de-industrialization of the United States by free trade.

I am not the only economist who takes issue with the free-trade dogma. A number of competent economists have criticized free-trade theory. For example, professors Herman E. Daly and John B. Cobb show the inadequacies of the theory in *For the Common Good* (1989). Professor James K. Galbraith puts the theory to rest in *The Predator State* (2008). Professor Robert E. Prasch, in a 1996 article in the *Review of Political Economy*, demonstrates fundamental problems with the theory. Professor Ron Baiman at DePaul University argues that Ricardo's theory is "mathematically over-determined and therefore generally unsolvable." Professor Michael Hudson deconstructs free trade doctrine in *Trade, Development and Foreign Debt* (2009) and in *America's Protectionist Takeoff 1815-1914* (2010). In 2004, America's most famous economist, Paul Samuelson, wrote that an improvement in the productivity of one country can decrease the living standard of another. Thus, when U.S. corporations take their technology abroad and integrate it into the productive capability of a foreign country, they reduce the living standards in their home country.

This brings us to Gomory and Baumol. Samuelson's 2004 article is a defense of the powerful new work in trade theory by these two authors. Gomory, one of America's most distinguished mathematicians, and Baumol, a past president of the American Economics Association, show that free-trade theory has many problems because "the modern free-trade world is so different from the original historical setting of the free-trade models."

Gomory and Baumol dismiss the alleged gains from offshoring production for home markets: "in almost all cases, most of the economic benefit stays where the value is added. Profits are usually only a small portion of the value added through economic activity, and most of the value added, such as wages, remains local. It matters to a country to be the site of an economic activity, whoever may own the company."

Gomory and Baumol show that unlike Ricardo's win-win outcome based on a simple arithmetical example, sophisticated mathematics proves that in most cases "the outcome [from trade] that is best for one country tends not to be good for another." Gomory and Baumol re-establish the gains from trade (win-win situation) as a special case of limited applicability. They conclude that "free trade between nations is not always and automatically beneficial. It can yield many stable equilibria in which a country is worse off than it would be if it isolated itself from trade altogether."

It will take the economics profession many years to come to terms with this new work. The myth that America's economic success is based on free trade will be hard to dislodge.

R.W. Thompson, in his *History of Protective Tariff Laws* (1888), shows that protectionism is the father of economic development. Free trade has become an ideology. It once had a Ricardian basis, a basis no longer present in the real world. In the United States today, "free trade" is a shield for greed. Short-term gains for management and shareholders are maximized at the expense of the labor force and the economic welfare of the country. Jobs offshoring is dismantling the ladders of upward mobility that made America an opportunity society.

Offshoring Exports Jobs Instead of Products

Offshoring's proponents defend the practice on the grounds that it is free trade and thereby beneficial.

We saw in the previous section that free trade is not necessarily beneficial. Let's now examine whether offshoring is trade.

In the traditional Ricardian free trade model, trade results from countries specializing in activities where they have comparative advantage and trading these products for the products of other countries doing likewise. In Ricardo's example, England specializes in woolen cloth and Portugal specializes in wine.

In the Ricardian model, *trade is not competitive.* English wool is not competing against Portuguese wool, and Portuguese wine is not competing against English wine.

Somewhere along the historical way, free trade became identified with competition between countries producing the same products. American TV sets vs. Japanese TV sets. American cars vs. Japanese cars. This meaning of free trade diverged from the Ricardian meaning based on comparative advantage and came to mean innovation and improvements in design and performance driven by foreign competition. Free trade became divorced from comparative advantage without the creation of a new theoretical basis upon which to base the free trade doctrine.

Countries competing against one another in the same array of products and services is not covered by Ricardian trade theory.

Offshoring doesn't fit the Ricardian or the competitive idea of free trade. In fact, offshoring is not trade.

Offshoring is the practice of a firm relocating its production of goods or services for its home market to a foreign country. When an American firm moves production offshore, US GDP declines by the amount of the offshored production, and foreign GDP increases by that amount. Employment and consumer income decline in the US and rise abroad. The US tax base shrinks, resulting in reductions in public services or in higher taxes or a switch from tax finance to bond finance and higher debt service cost.

When the offshored production comes back to the US to be marketed, the US trade deficit increases dollar for dollar. The trade deficit is financed by turning over to foreigners US assets and their future income streams. Profits, dividends, interest, capital gains, rents, and tolls from leased toll roads now flow from American pockets to foreign pockets, thus worsening the current account deficit as well.

Who benefits from these income losses suffered by Americans? Clearly, the beneficiary is the foreign country to which the production is moved. The other prominent beneficiaries are the shareholders and the executives of the companies that offshore production. The lower labor costs raise profits, the share price, and the "performance bonuses" of corporate management.

Offshoring's proponents claim that the lost incomes from job losses are offset by benefits to consumers from lower prices. Allegedly, the harm done to those who lose their jobs is more than offset by the benefit consumers in general get from the alleged lower prices. Yet, proponents are unable to cite studies that support this claim. The claim is based on the unexamined assumption that offshoring is free trade and, thereby, mutually beneficial.

Proponents of jobs offshoring also claim that the Americans who are left unemployed soon find equal or better jobs. This claim is based on the assumption that the demand for labor ensures full employment, and that people whose jobs have been moved abroad can be retrained for new jobs that are equal to or better than the jobs that were lost.

This claim is false. Offshoring affects *all* tradable goods and services. The nonfarm payroll data collected by the US Bureau of Labor Statistics makes clear that in the 21st century the US economy has been able to create net new jobs only in nontradable domestic services. Such employment is lowly paid compared to high value-added manufacturing jobs and professional services such as engineering. (Tradable goods and services are those that can be exported or that are substitutes for imports. Nontradable goods and services are those that only have domestic markets and no import competition. For example, barbers and dentists offer nontradable services.)

Moreover, even domestic services, such as school teachers and nurses, which cannot be offshored, can and are being performed by foreigners brought in on work visas.

The growing number of displaced and discouraged unemployed Americans is an external cost inflicted by offshoring firms on the displaced workers themselves, on taxpayers who provide unemployment and welfare benefits, and on the viability of the American political and economic system. The costs inflicted on the economy, taxpayers, and the displaced workers far exceeds the benefits to a few corporate executives and shareholders. The imposition of external costs on society in order to reward a very few is a powerful indication of the failure of laissez faire capitalism.

Some offshoring apologists go so far as to imply, and others even to claim, that offshore outsourcing is offset by "insourcing." For example, they point out that the Japanese have built car plants in the US. This is a false analogy. The Japanese car plants in the US are an example of direct foreign investment. The Japanese produce in the US in order to sell in the US. The plants are a response to Reagan era import quotas on Japanese cars and to high transport costs. The Japanese are not producing cars in the US for the purpose of sending them back to Japan to be marketed. They are not using cheaper American labor to produce for the Japanese home market. At least not yet.

However, as US wages are driven down by offshoring and work visas for foreigners, the US will find itself with an excess supply of labor that can, therefore, be employed at a wage less than labor's contribution to output. When this occurs, more prosperous countries, such as Japan, possibly could begin ruining their own economy by exporting jobs to Third World America.

Other apologists imply that H-1B and other work visas are a form of "insourcing." They argue that the ability of US firms to bring in foreigners to compensate for alleged shortages of US workers allows the corporations to keep their operations in America and not have to move them abroad. This false claim, which a March 2, 2009 *Washington Post* editorial endorsed, was rebutted by Senators Charles Grassley and Bernie Sanders, who observed that "with many thousands of financial services workers unemployed, it's absurd to claim that banks can't find top-notch American workers to perform these jobs" .

Senators Grassley and Sanders could have made a stronger point. The work visa program is supposed to be for specialized, high-tech skills that are allegedly in short-supply in the US. In fact, the vast majority of those brought in on work visas are brought in as lower-paid replacements for American workers, who are dismissed after being forced to train their foreign replacements.

The practice of replacing American employees with foreigners brought in on work visas is reported more at the state and local level than nationally. For example, on March 30, 2009, a Charlotte, North Carolina, TV station, WSOC, reported that Wachovia Bank (now Wells Fargo) was cutting labor costs by bringing in foreign replacements for American employees.

Congress forbade banks that receive bailout money from hiring foreigners to replace American employees. But the H-1B visa lobby got its hands on the legislation and inserted a loophole. The banks cannot directly hire foreigners as replacements for US employees, but they can hire contractors to supply "contract labor." The bank pays the contractor, and the contractor pays the workers.

On February 24, 2009, *Computerworld* reported that the H-1B visas are becoming the property of Indian contract labor firms, such as Tata, Infosys, Wipro, and Satyam.

These firms contract with American employers to supply reduced-cost labor from abroad with which to replace American employees.

The combination of offshoring and work visas is creating a new kind of American unemployment that cannot be cured by boosting consumer demand. *Business Week* (March 9, 2009) reports that JPMorgan Chase is increasing its outsourcing to India by 25 percent. *Computerworld* (February 24, 2009) reports that Nielsen Company, which measures TV audiences and consumer trends for clients, is laying off American employees at a Florida facility after announcing a 10-year global outsourcing agreement valued at $1.2 billion with Tata. *Computerworld* quotes Janice Miller, a city councilwoman: "they are still bringing in Indians, and there are a lot of local people out of work."

The New York Times (March 6, 2009) reports that IBM is laying off US employees piecemeal in order to avoid compliance with layoff notice laws. According to *The New York Times*, "IBM's American employment has declined steadily, down to 29 percent of its worldwide payroll."

The American population is being divorced from the production of the goods and services that they consume. It is the plight of a third world country to be dependent on goods and services that are not produced by its work force. The unaddressed question is how can Americans who are either unemployed or employed in low wage domestic services purchase the foreign made goods and services that are marketed to them?

If news reports are correct, even the lowest level

American jobs are subject to outsourcing. The fast food chain, McDonald's, is experimenting with having drive-up window orders routed to India via a VoIP internet connection. The person in India then posts the order to the kitchen and sends the billing to the cashier. If this works for McDonald's, the laid off software engineers, IT workers, and former bank employees will not even be able to get a job at a fast food restaurant.

Indeed, Americans already experience difficulty in finding restaurant jobs because of "insourcing." Young people from abroad are brought in on temporary visas and supplied by contractors to restaurants where they wait tables and do food prep work. In pharmacies, they serve as assistants. In grocery stores they are employed as checkout clerks. Mexicans have a large share of construction and agricultural jobs. Americans are finding occupation after occupation closed to them.

The United States is unable to deal with its serious economic problems, because powerful interest groups benefit from the continuation of the problems. As long as narrow private interests can cloak themselves in free trade's claim of increased general welfare, the American economy will continue its relative and absolute decline, and American taxpayers will continue to bear the cost of workers displaced by offshoring and work visas.

The Problem of External Costs

Prices are efficient allocators of resources only if prices reflect all costs of production. In theoretical writings, economists have dealt extensively with "external costs," which are costs that the producer does not incur but which are imposed on third parties. However, in the real world external costs are a large and growing problem. Often what economists and businesses describe as "lowest cost production" is production that imposes very large costs on third parties, costs that are not reflected in the prices of the products. These "external" or "social costs" of production are costs that businesses inflict on society.

Regulation is one way of dealing with external costs. However, as economist George Stigler pointed out several decades ago, regulatory agencies are captured by the industries that they regulate. Stigler could have added that universities and research institutes financed with industry funds are also captured. Therefore, both regulation and studies of its effects have proven to be imperfect tools for controlling external costs.

Information is coming to light that genetically modified seeds such as those that produce crops resistant to herbicides, thus lowering the cost of weed control, have massive external costs. In 2011 Purdue University professor Don Huber, a plant pathologist and soil microbiologist, wrote to the US Secretary of Agriculture about the unintended consequences of GMOs. Among these are adverse effects on critical micronutrients, soil fertility, and the nutritional value of foods. The impairment of metabolic pathways that is associated with GMOs prevents the ability of plants to accumulate and to store minerals, such as iron, manganese, and zinc that are important for liver function and immune response in animals and people.

Toxic effects on the microorganisms in the soil have disrupted nature's balance. One result has been a sharp increase in plant diseases. Another is livestock deaths from botulism. Yet another is a sharp increase in animal reproductive problems. And another is premature animal aging.

As the human diet has transitioned to GMO crops and meat produced with genetically modified, corn, soybeans, and alfalfa, there has been a sharp rise in human infertility.

In an interview, Professor Huber said that the power of Monsanto and agri-business has made it almost impossible to do research on GMOs, that we are flying blind, and might be in the process of killing ourselves. Regulatory agencies are dependent on the industry's own studies and have no independent objective science on which to base a regulatory decision.[3]

If we add up the external costs of GMOs—reduced nutritional value, rise in plant and animal disease, human and animal reproductive problems, and other problems of which we might not be aware—it seems obvious that the external costs are far greater than the savings from the lower cost of production made possible by herbicide resistant crops.

Another problem with herbicide resistant crops is the active ingredient, glyphosate, in Monsanto's Roundup herbicide with which the GMO crops are sprayed. According to the US Environmental Protection Agency, 30 grams of glyphosate is a fatal dose for adults.

The Internet site OpEdNews reported on December 22, 2011, that a new study in the journal, *Analytical and Bioanalytical Chemistry*, reported that 41% of 140 groundwater samples taken from Catalonia, Spain, contained unexpected levels of glyphosate. This is an indication that glyphosate is accumulating in the environment instead of breaking down.[4]

The US Geological Survey reports that glyphosate is now "commonly found in rain and streams in the Mississippi River Basin."[5] Considering the toxic effects of glyphosate, the external costs of GMO crops might be unprecedented in scale.

Energy production is a source of large external costs. The BP oil spill in the Gulf of Mexico, for example, destroyed fisheries and soiled beaches, leading to income losses for large numbers of people. People who lost income from the spill received some monetary compensation, but the natural environment remains polluted. Nature does not have a representative and, therefore, becomes the depository for the wastes of profit making corporations.

Untreated acid discharges from coal mining have made many streams lifeless. Fracking, a new process by which huge amounts of water with chemical additives are pumped into the earth to aid the extraction of oil and gas, together with discharges from coal mining, have created high salinity levels in which golden algae (prymnesium parvum) thrives. This algae destroys all aquatic life. The costs of polluted streams and destroyed aquatic life are external to the corporations that inflict the costs.[6]

Another external cost of fracking is the drop in water levels of streams when water is withdrawn for use in fracking operations. The drop in water flows make the streams less able to survive pollution from other sources.

Pollution from energy production is not limited to America. It is worldwide. Amnesty International (Fall/Winter, 2011) reports that between 9 and 13 million barrels of oil have been spilled in the Niger Delta region of Nigeria by the multinational petroleum industry. Fishing and farming communities have been devastated. The Nigerian government is bought-and-paid-for and, thus, fails to hold accountable the international corporations,

Some other examples will help to illustrate the nature of external costs. A half-century ago, in his book, *The Federal Bulldozer*, Martin Anderson pointed out that urban renewal was a means for liberals to gentrify their cities with federal money at the expense of ethnic neighborhoods and housing for the poor. Anderson was right, but federal spending programs had acquired a moral status that protected them from inconvenient facts. Indeed, today the right of developers to profit by imposing costs on others is more sacrosanct than the Bill of Rights.

In 2009 a developer in Dawson County, Georgia, succeeded in getting the Dawsonville City Council to rezone 150 acres of rural residential land as commercial/ industrial. The developer intends to construct a motorsports race track amid horse farms, wildlife management areas, and low density residential use. The maneuvering began with Dawsonville annexing the land, thus preventing the county from protecting the property owners who invested in a tranquil way of life that the developer and obedient city council have conspired to destroy.

The developer's profits and the tax revenues he has promised the small town of Dawsonville will not reflect the heavy costs his project imposes on residents in an environment where property values depend on natural beauty and peace and quiet.

In economic jargon, the developer is generating external costs that do not factor into his assessment of the value of his project. The costs are external to the project, because they are imposed on others. The project assigns no value to the quality of life that it destroys.

A fair-minded person would say that the developer should not be allowed to proceed unless he compensates those whose tranquility his project disrupts and whose property values it harms. Compensation would raise the cost of the project and perhaps make it unprofitable. Many economists, however, especially free market ideologues, will say that if the residents do not want the project they should pay the developer the present value of his expected profits not to go forward with the project.

Obviously, a policy of buying off the developer would bring in another with an even more outrageous project in order to extract higher blackmail.

Historically, free market economists have been inclined to see the property rights *of the developer* as sacrosanct. The property rights of existing owners in tranquility, low density, unobstructed views, and clean air are treated as expendable.

Zoning is society's way of protecting property investments from reclassification that would harm their values. But zoning has proven an unreliable instrument as property developers usually prevail over communities. The Dawsonville city council changed the rules after residents had made their commitments and after the area had developed in keeping with the original zoning. Such zoning changes, if permitted at all, should be illegal without a two-thirds or three-fourths vote of the residents. Politicians can be swayed by bribes or promises of increased tax revenues. Consequently, politicians often place special interests above the general interest.

Free market ideologues are opposed to zoning because it protects existing commitments by limiting the rights of a new entrant. Free market ideologues believe that a person has the right to establish a pig farm in the middle of a residential neighborhood or a porn shop next to a church or a half-way house for drug addicts next to an elementary school. Otherwise, the state is interfering with property rights, which means that land is not being put to its most valued use as measured by the profits of the project, profits that are not offset by the costs the project imposes on others.

Developers are notorious for imposing high costs on taxpayers. Some local jurisdictions now require developers to put in curbs, sidewalks, water and sewage. However, many costs of development projects are still passed on to taxpayers.

Consider Walton County in the Florida panhandle. Federal Reserve chairman Alan Greenspan's unrealistic low interest rates and environmental complaints about St. Joe's paper mill caused the company to put its vast land holdings into real estate development. The paper company owned miles of undeveloped land along the coast of the Gulf of Mexico and hundreds of thousands of acres inland. These vast holdings that had provided pulp wood for the paper mill and habitat for wildlife became locations for vacation homes and shopping centers.

In less than a decade density increased to the degree that hurricane evacuation became impossible. Taxpayers were shouldered with the cost of turning two-lane roads into four-lane roads and two-lane bridges into four-lane bridges, eventually reaching Interstate-10 seventy miles away. Even if St. Joe had been required to pay this cost, the homes and businesses and small towns along the two-lane highway are forever destroyed. A way of life is gone forever, and no one was compensated.

On the national level, financial interests, the military/security complex, and the American Israel Public Affairs Committee (AIPAC) rule. On the state and local level real estate developers rule. This is especially the case in Florida where campaign contributions insure that city and county commissions will approve development plans that destroy the natural environment and local communities.

The destruction of Florida by real estate developers is now so extreme that aroused residents organized an initiative for the November 2010 ballot known as Florida Hometown Democracy. The initiative would require all approved changes in growth plans to be decided by voters in referendums in the affected communities. The real estate lobby used its financial resources to fund a campaign of disinformation that defeated the initiative, thus retaining its ability to externalize its costs.

Economists opposed Florida Hometown Democracy as an interference with private property rights that would divert land resources "from their most productive use." Floridians need to keep in mind that economists measure "most productive use" by profits that are created by imposing costs of the projects on those who suffer from them. If the full costs were imposed on the projects, fewer would be undertaken.

Real estate developers are infamous for naming their "developments" after the vistas they destroy. "Oak Hill," for example, will be a hillside subdivision where a forest of oaks once stood. "Walnut Mill Run" memorializes the swift running stream that is now encased in galvanized pipe buried in the backyards of the houses built on the site.

It is easy to beat up real estate developers for their destruction of natural habitat, but they are not the worst generators of external costs. I cannot say which profit-making entity deserves that crown. Externalities generated by the high-density factory farming of meat and eggs might prove to be the most dangerous to humans.

American farm soils are depleted, and crops now depend on chemical fertilizers, the run-off from which destroys water resources. The factory farming of animals produces dangerous viruses, such as the H1N1 swine flu virus, which first emerged in the late 1980s from intensive pork production in North Carolina and recently was thought to be threatening the world with a pandemic originating in a subsidiary of Smithfield Farms in Mexico. The "low-cost" production of pork does not include the deaths and illnesses, the expense of treatment, lost incomes and grief suffered by families.

The meat that Americans eat is produced in the most inhumane conditions imaginable. No science fiction could do the production process justice. The animals exist in dangerous germ pools in such deplorable conditions that they must be pumped full of antibiotics. I know people who are not vegetarians who refuse to eat meat because of the inhumane, "low-cost," conditions in which it is produced.

The same goes for the production of eggs and poultry. There is little doubt that the bird flu virus is a product of the inhumane conditions under which "low-cost" protein is produced.

Unfortunately in America, economists believe that "low-cost" production is the be-all and end-all of "consumer satisfaction." Until economists, or preferably people in society, realize that in economic jargon "low-cost" production might simply mean maximum external costs imposed on society and the environment, the vaunted unregulated market economy will continue on its path toward the destruction of life on earth.

Nature's Capital

So far we have dealt with economics within the existing paradigm. This section deals with the economics that is omitted from the paradigm. The omitted economics is so important that the omission indicates the need for a new economic paradigm.

As we have seen, a basic problem is that economics does not measure all the costs, and the omitted costs might be the most important costs. Since economics does not measure all the costs, economists cannot know whether growth is economic or uneconomic. Economist Herman Daly, for example, asks if the ecological and social costs of growth have grown larger than the value of the increase in production.

The costs that are left out of the computation of Gross Domestic Product are the depletion of natural capital, such as oil and mineral resources and fisheries, and the pollution of air, water and land resources.

Economists do a poor job of adjusting economic theory to developments brought by the passage of time. Just as capital theory originated prior to the income tax and free-trade theory originated at a period in history when capital was internationally immobile and tradable goods were based on climate and knowledge differences, economists' neglect of the ecosystem as a finite, entropic, non-growing and materially closed system dates from an earlier "empty world."

In an empty world, man-made capital is scarce and nature's capital is plentiful. In an empty world, the fish catch is limited by the number of fishing boats, not by the remaining fish population, and petroleum energy is limited by drilling capability, not by geological deposits. Empty-world economics focuses on the sustainability of man-made capital, not on natural capital. Natural capital is treated as a free good. Using it up is not treated as a cost but as an increase in output.

Economic theory is based on "empty-world" economics. But, in fact, today the world is full. In a "full world," the fish catch is limited by the remaining population of fish, not by the number of fishing boats, which are man-made capital in excess supply. Oil energy is limited by geological deposits, not by the drilling and pumping capacity of man-made capital. In national income accounting, the use of man-made capital is depreciated, but the use of nature's capital has no cost other than extraction cost. Therefore, the using up of natural capital always results in economic growth.

For example, the dead zones in the Gulf of Mexico from fertilizer runoff from chemical fertilizer farming are not counted as a cost against the increase in agricultural output from chemical farming. The brown clouds that reduce light over large areas of Asia are not included as costs in the production of energy from coal. Economists continue to assume that the only limits to growth are labor, man-made capital, and consumer demand. In fact, the critical limit is ecological.

Nature's resources cannot be replicated or regenerated like man-made capital. These real limits to growth are both neglected and denied by economic theory.

Modern economics is based on a "production function," associated with Robert Solow and Joseph Stiglitz, two Nobel prizewinners. A production function explains the relationship between inputs and outputs. The Solow-Stiglitz production function assumes that man-made capital is a substitute for nature's capital. Therefore, as long as man-made capital can be reproduced, there are no limits to growth. As the economists James Tobin (another Nobel prizewinner) and William Nordhaus put it in 1972, the implicit assumption is that "reproducible [man-made] capital is a near perfect substitute for land and other exhaustible resources."

Nicholas Georgescu-Roegen, one of the world's most distinguished mathematical economists (now deceased) dismissed the Solow-Stiglitz production function as a "conjuring trick." However, economists have continued to rely on the Solow-Stiglitz production function, because it rules out ecological limits on economic growth.[7]

Modern economics has turned economic growth into an ideology, just as free trade has become an ideology. The Solow-Stiglitz production function is a false explanation of how inputs produce outputs. In contrast with Solow-Stiglitz, Georgescu-Roegen made it clear that production is the transformation of resources into useful products and into waste products. Labor and man-made capital are agents of transformation, while natural resources are what are transformed into useful products and waste products. Man-made capital and natural capital are complements, not substitutes. Neither can serve as a replacement for the other. The Solow-Stiglitz production function, the basis of modern economics, is fantasy.

The real question is whether the world's remaining

natural resources and the "sinks" for waste products are sufficient to sustain the continuation of economic growth as traditionally understood and its expansion to underdeveloped countries. Interest groups promise to unlock endless resources with new technologies. Currently proponents of fracking are promising Americans 100 years of energy independence. This claim is propaganda designed to convince Americans to accept water contamination so that fracking companies can pull in short-term profits. Writing in Global Research on March 13, 2013, William Engdahl shows that fracking claims are "a gigantic hyped confidence bubble that is already beginning to deflate." Steve Horn writing in *Counterpunch* on February 20, 2013, reports that shale gas is a bubble whipped up into a frenzy by Wall Street. The false hopes generated by false claims prevent recognition that nature's capital is a constraint on economic growth.

Environmentalists and ecological economists are aware that today the limits to growth include the natural environment. Ecological economists stress "steady-state economics." The focus of steady-state economics is to maintain living standards into the future. The ruthless exploitation of nature's capital sacrifices the long-run sustainability of life in order to raise the consumption levels for a few generations. The depletion of natural resources and the pollution of air, water, and soil bite back in the end, and the ability of the planet to sustain life collapses.

"Steady-state economics" permits growth that is produced by developments in science and technology and better agricultural practices. This growth would be muted but sustainable compared to growth that depends on the exhaustion of natural resources and the pollution of the planet.

Most of the Western population would not notice the change to steady-state economics. The traditional notion of economic growth no longer works for the bulk of the population. For example, in the US there has been no growth in the real incomes of the vast bulk of the population for several decades. Households have maintained "steady-state" income by putting both husband and wife in the work force. Two people now provide the real income formerly provided by one, so the "growth model" no longer works. The growth model today in the West only serves the 1%.

The growth model works in China and India because of the relocation of First World economic activity to those countries. Thus, Chinese incomes rise, while US incomes fall. In other non-western lands, the growth model destroys sustainable economic life and substitutes in its place monocultures. Consequently, countries where life was sustainable now have to import their food.

Over the course of American history, economic growth has made income inequality acceptable, because economic growth, as President John F. Kennedy put it, is "a tide that lifts all boats." What becomes of a society based on the rise in real incomes when ecology imposes its limits? Can costs that outweigh the benefits be forever ignored?

Can a society, which is based on children doing better economically than their parents, survive when policy mistakes, such as offshoring, together with ecological exhaustion disrupt this traditional outcome?

Just as there are social costs associated with the failure of economics to account for the full costs of production, there are social costs associated with the integration of all countries into a "global economy." For many countries, being integrated into the global economy means that the society loses control over itself. Entire occupations and ways of life are destroyed as specific countries are forced to forego diversification and to specialize in the products that globalism dictates, regardless of the needs and wants of the domestic population.

Economic globalism is far in advance of global government. As Herman Daly writes, globalism is the "space into which transnational corporations move to escape regulation by national governments." Economic globalism in the absence of global government permits transnational corporations to escape accountability.

This means that today corporations are escaping accountability for costs that they impose on the rest of the world. If these "externalized" costs were included in their cost of production, would there be any basis for CEOs to be paid 300, 400, or 500 times the pay of a production employee?

If ecology imposes limits on growth, ladders of upward mobility cease to function. How would society distribute income in order to ensure social peace? This new distribution would certainly require the end of the current large inequality in income and wealth, but would people be locked into place, requiring luck and extraordinary ability to rise?

In the founding days of the discipline of economics, Adam Smith and Alfred Marshall endeavored to explain reality in order that policy might improve the human condition. Whether they succeeded or failed, they were sincere. Today, economists create artificial reality with assumptions and equations. Smith and Marshall were interested in truth and its discovery. Economists today are interested in money, and they provide apologies for "globalism" that bring grants to their university departments from transnational corporations. Today a person who speaks economic truth has no future in the economics department of a university dependent on outside money.

If economics is to serve humankind, the limits imposed by ecological resources must be acknowledged. Externalities are not very important in an "empty world," but in a "full world" ignored externalities can offset the value of increased output. When the last species is gone, how is it replaced? How are exhausted natural resources replenished and the climate reclaimed? To treat resources created by nature over millions of years as devoid of costs other than the costs of extraction is absurd. If economics is to be of any use to humanity, it must cease being absurd.

Planning for a Full World

If humankind is to contend successfully with depleting natural capital, planning will be required. In their book, *Ecological Economics: Principles and Applications*, Herman Daly and J. Farley point out that in the 20th century both the Soviet Union and the US had economic growth as their first priority. In the Soviet Union, Marx's "new socialist man" would appear only with the disappearance of scarcity, which required the maximum growth in output. In the US high growth was seen as the best way to avoid class conflict by producing a larger pie to divide.

Despite their vaunted mathematics, economists have failed to understand that infinite growth in a finite system is impossible. The Soviet economy failed first, because its gross output indicator was more inefficient than the price and profit indicators used in the West.

The West saw Soviet economic failure as proof of market capitalism's superiority. This conclusion was correct up to a point, but the "end of history" euphoria neglected the real end of history implicit in the exhaustion of environmental capital. For organized human society to deal with the consequences of this exhaustion, planning is essential. But planning is discredited by Soviet failure.

Fortunately, the planning required bears no resemblance to Soviet planning, which was ideological in origin. As I proved in my book, *Alienation and the Soviet*

Economy (1971, 1990), the purpose of Soviet planning was to eliminate the market and the price and profit signals upon which it relies, and to organize the entire economy as if it were a self-sufficient farm producing for its own use. In a modern economy with large numbers of input and output combinations, this is a strict impossibility. Marxian central economic planning is simply not achievable. This is not the kind of planning needed to stave off societal collapse from environmental exhaustion.

Despite the inefficiency of its gross output success indicator, the Soviet economy had features that insulated citizens to some degree from economic breakdown. It would be worthwhile to incorporate some of these features in the organization of the US economy. In 2006 Dmitry Orlov identified some of these features when he compared the Soviet economic collapse with a future US economic collapse and concluded that Soviet citizens were better positioned to survive economic disruption.

One large difference is America's dependence on depleting water and energy resources, especially petroleum energy in which it is not self-sufficient. In contrast, Soviet Russia was energy self-efficient, and today Russia is an exporter of energy.

Despite being energy self-sufficient, Soviet Russia was not dependent on an automobile economy. Russians could meet their occupational and shopping needs with public transportation.

Occupants of Soviet housing, as bad as it was, were not subject to mortgage foreclosures and homelessness.

Soviet citizens were inured to hardships and accustomed to bartering for their needs.

Soviet families tended to be in the same place and supportive. U.S. families are widely scattered and less able to come to one another's help.

Soviet appliances could be repaired. American ones are disposable. Thus, a shut-down of imports has different consequences in the U.S. than in the USSR.

Despite the notorious failure of Soviet agriculture, basic foodstuffs—cabbages, onions, potatoes—were close at hand. Many residents of cities had access to garden plots. The largest metropolitan areas had surrounding agricultural areas. In the U.S. food is trucked in from vast distances. Garden plots are rare outside of rural areas.

Soviet medicine focused on prevention with immunization programs, infectious disease control, and basic care. The state-run clinics and hospitals were not profit-based. In the U.S. health care is a profit system in which doctors refuse to diagnose, instead ordering expensive tests in order to protect themselves against liability claims. If profits leave the system, financing collapses.

My summary barely does justice to Orlov. But the point comes across. The U.S., unlike the former Soviet Union, is import-dependent for energy and manufactured goods. Americans are dependent on private cars for access to their jobs, food, and medical care. A disruption in gasoline supply automatically disrupts food deliveries to stores and the ability of the work force to show up for work. Americans are not inured to hardship and lack survival skills.

The development pattern of the U.S. was based on abundant and cheap gasoline. Urban areas became huge metropolitan areas of suburban sprawl, with people traveling large distances on a daily basis in order to commute to their jobs and shop for their needs. The man hours lost in commuting are substantial.

Surplus U.S. food stocks that were the products of agricultural subsidy programs have been eliminated. Agriculture is increasingly concentrated in large factory farms, whether for grains or meat. Even dairy farms are falling into concentrated hands. Food output is increasingly centralized in locations distant from most cities. A transportation disruption will disrupt food distribution. The crowded and unsanitary conditions in which meat and eggs are produced permit the rapid spread of diseases that could decimate food production.

If the future is left to take care of itself, organized society in the U.S. could fail.

Risks could be minimized by giving thought to the energy implications of suburban development and perhaps subsidize, if necessary, food production near population concentrations. Development plans could be required to specify the water resources. Public transportation systems could be created that can be run by renewable energy. All measures that reduce the rate of exhaustion of nature's resources and preserve the U.S. dollar as world reserve currency are useful forms of planning.

The problem with planning is not only government inefficiency, but also the power of organized interest groups to use planning to elevate their interests above those of society. Much thought would have to be given to preventing planning from becoming just another tool of interest groups. Perhaps giving key roles to bodies of independent experts and scientists could mitigate the political corruption, assuming there are still any experts and scientists who are independent and not corruptible.

There is no doubt that the efforts of humans, being imperfect creatures, to plan for life in a full world would be beset with errors and miscalculations. But however imperfect the product would be, the result would be better than what must result from the economists' assumption that man-made capital is a perfect substitute for nature's capital and that, therefore, resources are inexhaustible. To conclude that our future is a continuation of the past is a death warrant for society.

Failures of Economic Theory Are Pervasive

The failures of economic theory and the disastrous consequences that result from applying failed theories to policy are more extensive than those I have related. My account is selective in order to emphasize that globalism is a mechanism for bringing poverty to the First World, while accelerating the economic development of India and China.

There is a great deal of failure in economic theory and policy, and the failures punish both rich and poor countries alike. Some thoughtful economists interpret the theory on which International Monetary Fund (IMF) structural adjustment programs are based as a conspiracy of the First World against the Third World. Structural adjustment imposes economic distress on Third World populations in order to direct income flows to First World creditors and corporations.[8] But the same theory that imposes austerity on the world's poorest people is also wrecking the prospects of First World labor.

Consider what is known variously as the Heckscher-Ohlin theorem, Heckscher-Ohlin trade theory, or Heckscher-Ohlin factor endowment theory. (By "factor endowment" economists mean a country's supplies of land, labor, and capital. Capital refers to technology embodied in machinery.) This theory assumes that every country's land, labor, and capital resources are as productive as every other country's. What, then, accounts for countries having international cost advantages? According to the theory, cost advantage is based on countries having different abundances (larger or smaller supplies) of the three factors of production.

The implication of this theory for international trade is that countries with the largest supply of capital should focus on producing capital-intensive goods for export; those with the largest supply of labor should focus on labor-intensive goods; those with the most land should focus on agriculture or extractive industries such as mining.

Among the theory's assumptions is that land, labor, and capital provide unique contributions to production and, thus, cannot take the place of one another. The production of each product has its own ratio of land, labor, and capital. Thus, capital is not competitive with labor and is not a substitute for it.

One implication of this theory is that increased US capital investment in China, for example, cannot result in the displacement or unemployment of US labor. As we will see, US policymakers following this theory have wrecked the economic prospects for US labor.

A conclusion drawn from this theory by Paul Samuelson is known as the factor-price equalization theorem. This theorem says that free trade will cause wages, rents, and profits to equalize in every country. We do not need to examine this theorem beyond its implication for First World labor. The excess supply of labor in China and India today exceeds the total of the employed labor forces of the US and Europe. How far will US and European wages have to fall in order to become equalized with Chinese and Indian wages?

Heckscher-Ohlin theory locks poor countries into labor-intensive and agricultural/mineral production at the expense of capital investments that would raise the productivity of labor and wages in those countries. When the IMF imposes structural adjustment programs on indebted poor countries, the IMF follows Heckscher-Ohlin theory, which mandates labor-intensive and agricultural production as the path to progress for Third World countries. Part of the IMF's structural adjustment menu consists of free trade and privatization. Free trade or "trade liberalization" prevents a country from protecting its "infant industries" in order that they can develop. Privatization generally transfers a country's resources from its control to that of First World corporations. Thus, the country is blocked from the path of development and becomes a source of cheap labor and raw materials.

The theory's predicted convergence of wages, rents, and profits across countries is not occurring. Moreover, the rapidly rising economies of China and India are not following the Heckscher-Ohlin prescriptions. Instead, China and India are investing in manufacturing and in tradable professional skills, and their development has received a large boost from jobs offshoring by US and European corporations.

Instead of equalizing as Heckscher-Ohlin theory predicts, income is concentrating in fewer hands. Those hands are mainly the hands of powerful Western financial institutions, especially American ones, that with deregulation and concentration have acquired the ability to manipulate prices in equity, bond, currency, and commodity markets.

The ability that large financial institutions have acquired to accumulate income and wealth is due in part to the simplifying assumption in economic theory that treats all participants in the economic process—consumers and corporations, large and small businesses, farmers and financiers—as having equal influence, with no participant able to influence the market. The assumption that "markets are self-regulating," an assumption that was transformed into US economic policy, resulted in the financial crisis that began in 2008 and is ongoing. This assumption is based on the belief that no corporation or economic sector has the political power to commit fraud or has the economic power to game, rig, or manipulate markets.

The failures of economic theory have resulted in the failure of capitalism. Capitalism no longer allocates resources efficiently or equitably. Profits are no longer a measure of social welfare. The claim made by economists that capitalism serves social welfare is no longer true.

The Failure of Laissez Faire Capitalism

Problematic economic doctrines, such as free trade and the deteriorating information content of price and profit signals caused by rising external costs and shrinking natural capital, indicate that empty world economics no longer suffices. We need a new economics for a full world.

Economists will resist such change, because of their investments of their human capital in empty world economics. Status, position, and income flow from one's stake in the existing economics corpus. Economists will keep a blind eye turned as long as they can.

However, as subsequent sections of this book will illustrate, time is running out for economics as we have known it. Not only have the resurrection of laissez faire capitalism and the claim that markets are self-regulating failed, but also the two main justifications of market capitalism have been destroyed by the emergence of financial institutions that are "too big to fail" and by jobs offshoring. If markets do not eliminate failures, then capitalism's claim to efficiently allocate resources is undermined. If profits are not a measure of a society's welfare, the justification for profit maximization no longer exists. The theoretical edifice that associates capitalism with social welfare collapses. The purpose of this section is to make that clear.

The economic and financial mess in which the US and Europe find themselves and which has been exported to much of the rest of the world is the *direct consequence of too much economic freedom*. The excess freedom is the direct consequence of financial deregulation.

The definition of free markets is ambiguous. At times it means a market without any regulation. In other cases it means markets in which prices are free to reflect supply and demand. Sometimes it means competitive markets free of monopoly or concentration. Free market economists have made a mistake by elevating an economy that is free of regulation as the ideal. This ideological position overlooks that regulation can increase economic efficiency and that without regulation external costs can offset the value of production.

Before going further, let's be clear about what is regulated. Economists reify markets: the market did this, the market did that. But the market is not an actor. The market is a social institution. People act, and it is the behavior of people that is regulated. When free market economists describe the ideal as the absence of any regulation of economic behavior, they are asserting that there are no dysfunctional consequences of unregulated economic behavior.

If this were in fact the case, why should this result be confined to economic behavior? Why should not all human behavior be unregulated? Why is it that economists recognize that robbery, rape, and murder are socially dysfunctional, but fail to see unlimited debt leverage and misrepresentation of financial instruments as socially dysfunctional? The claim, as expressed by former Federal Reserve chairman Alan Greenspan along with others, that "markets are self-regulating" is an assertion that unrestrained individuals are self-regulating. How did anyone ever believe that?

When Federal Reserve Chairman Alan Greenspan, Treasury Secretary Robert Rubin, Deputy Treasury Secretary Larry Summers, and SEC Chairman Arthur Levitt browbeat Brooksley Born, head of the Commodity Future Trading Corporation, and prevented her from doing her duty to regulate over-the-counter derivatives, we witnessed either the four most stupid public officials in human history or four crooks setting up a new scam for Wall Street.

The financial crisis that resulted has spread its devastating effects everywhere. The explosions in public debt and money creation, which have resulted from efforts to bail out the financial system from its own stupidity and greed, have brought the US dollar and the euro, the two reserve currencies of the international financial system, under pressure, threatening the reserve currency status of the currencies and the international financial system with collapse.

Obviously, the lack of financial regulation was dysfunctional in the extreme, and the social costs of the policy error are enormous.

Thirty-three years ago in an article in the *Journal of Monetary Economics* (August 1978), "Idealism in Public Choice Theory," I presented a model to assess the benefits and costs of regulation. I argued that well-thought-out regulation could be a factor of production that increases Gross National Product. For example, regulation that contributes to the quality and safety of food and medicines encourages specialization in production and lower costs, and regulations enforcing contracts and private property rights add to economic efficiency.

On the other hand bureaucracies build their empires and extend their regulations into the realm of negative returns. Moreover, as regulations increase, economic managers spend more time in red tape and less in productive activity. As rules proliferate, they become contradictory and result in paralysis.

I had hopes that my analysis would result in a more thoughtful approach to regulation, but to no avail. Partisans of larger government continued to argue that more regulation was better, and libertarians maintained than none was best.

The ongoing financial crisis has given us a taste of what the absence of regulation can produce. Despite the enormous cost, the financial system remains unregulated. As soon as Wall Street devises a new financial instrument and finds new suckers, the debacle will again happen.

The ambiguous concept of freedom in economics has laid other minefields. Until the Clinton administration, economic concentration was seen as impinging on economic freedom. As late as the Reagan administration, AT&T was broken up. The Clinton administration permitted the concentration of the media. Formerly, this concentration would not only have been considered "in restraint of trade," but also contrary to the American tradition of a diverse and independent press. Today mergers and concentration of economic power are no longer seen as encroachments on competitive markets but as necessary to maintain global competitiveness. In the George W. Bush and Obama administrations, we have witnessed enormous financial concentrations.

One consequence has been that financial corporations can no longer be held accountable as they "are too big to fail." Thus, the economists' story of how the market weeds out the failures can no longer be told. The failures accumulate and are subsidized with public money. *This is the antithesis of economic efficiency.*

The dispersed power that made the market a socially functional institution is disappearing. For example, capital is free to concentrate, but labor unions, a "countervailing power" to capital, are being destroyed. Jobs offshoring has destroyed the manufacturing unions, and now politicians are using the state and local budget crises to destroy public sector unions. Unbridled capitalism, no longer restrained by regulation or by countervailing power, has reemerged. The Robber Barons have been resurrected.

Developments since the collapse of the Soviet Union twenty years ago have confused economists and produced results that threaten the edifice of economic theory. Economists have confused jobs offshoring with free trade. However, as we have seen, jobs offshoring is not trade at all. It is labor arbitrage. Free trade theory is based on comparative advantage. Labor arbitrage is the pursuit of absolute advantage.

Profits resulting from jobs offshoring raise questions about economic theory's justification of profit maximization. Theoretically, profits are justified, because they are evidence that resources were efficiently used in producing consumer satisfaction and are a measure of the economic welfare of the society. *This conclusion no longer holds when profits are produced by rendering a country's work force unemployed.* Offshoring separates consumers from the incomes and careers associated with the production of the goods and services that they consume. The profits from offshoring reflect the economic welfare of the foreign country. Therefore, the edifice that economists have built that justifies market capitalism as the deliverer of economic welfare to society no longer stands.

PART II

THE NEW DISPOSSESSION

Class war is raging in the US and Europe. It is the political elites and the monied interests that control them against everyone else. In the US class war of the "one percent" against the "99 percent" created the Occupy Wall Street (OWS) movement as a response from the "99 percent." In Europe it has brought citizens into the streets in Greece, Spain, and Italy.

The dispossession of the people has gone beyond economic dispossession; citizens are being dispossessed socially and politically as well. The US is no longer a model of "freedom and democracy." Citizens have been stripped of representative government and the Constitution's guarantee of civil liberty. Citizens who still vote find that the ballot box is unable to bring change.

Americans have been dispossessed politically, because (1) they have lost representative government, (2) they have lost the accountability of government to law, and (3) they have lost their civil liberties that protected them from a police state and the use of law as a weapon by government.

Americans have been dispossessed economically, because (1) millions of middle class jobs have been moved offshore to China, India, and other low wage locations, (2) the burden of massive losses in the financial sector has been placed on taxpayers and on the US dollar's credibility as world reserve currency, and (3) continued high immigration and work visas for foreigners further impair the ability of unemployed Americans to find a job.

Americans have been dispossessed socially, because (1) the ladders of upward mobility have been dismantled, (2) a university education is no longer a path to a middle class existence, (3) millions have lost their homes and careers, (4) median income has been falling for a number of years, and (5) the income and wealth distribution is now so skewed toward the top that a small number of people control the wealth, the income that wealth produces, and the political power that money buys.

I will discuss these elements of dispossession in the order in which they are listed.

Political Dispossession

Elected representatives are unresponsive to voters. Election outcomes are almost always determined by money. Therefore, representatives are responsive to those who provide their campaign funds. Seldom are these people the voters. Campaign funds are provided by interest groups, such as Wall Street, the military-security complex, agri-business, the American Israel Public Affairs Committee, and large corporations in general. In 2010 the US Supreme Court ruled that it is merely the exercise of free speech, a constitutionally protected right, when powerful corporations purchase the US government with campaign donations.

This "protected right" is not protected for war protesters and other dissidents, as we will see.

President Richard Nixon was the last US president

to be held accountable to law. There was an unsuccessful effort to hold President Bill Clinton accountable. However, the George W. Bush administration succeeded in elevating the president above the law. President Bush succeeded in violating the Foreign Intelligence Surveillance Act (FISA) and spied on Americans without obtaining warrants from the FISA court.

Bush also succeeded in violating both US and international laws against torture. In placing the president above the law, the Bush administration had the help of the Federalist Society, an organization of Republican lawyers who believe that the president has unique powers that place executive decisions above the reach of the legislature and the courts.

By failing to hold Bush and officials of his administration accountable for their unambiguous violations of law, the Obama administration has, in effect, accepted the constitutional coup that has elevated the president above the law. The American president is now a Caesar.

The transformation of the president into a caesar coincided with "the war on terror." The Bush regime used fear created by the "terrorist threat" to deny to detainees and accused people both constitutional protections and the protections of the Geneva Conventions. Initially, it was only foreign "enemy combatants" who were held without due process. However, accused American citizens soon found themselves denied habeas corpus, right to an attorney, and due process.[9] Unconstitutional laws, such as the PATRIOT Act, were passed to provide legal cover for constitutional violations by the executive branch.

A massive new federal police agency, Homeland Security, was created in 2002 to protect Americans from a non-existent "terrorist threat." By 2011 this federal police agency had shifted its focus from terrorists to "domestic extremists," defined as war protesters, environmentalists, animal rights activists, and everyone else of whom elites disapprove. In 2011 FBI agents burst into the homes of peace activists in Michigan, North Carolina, Wisconsin and other states seizing the residents' computers and other possessions that could possibly be misconstrued as evidence in behalf of the charge that the peace activists had given material support to foreign terrorist organizations by opposing America's wars.[10] Federal grand juries were convened in efforts to indict peace activists under terrorism laws.

The government is working to shut down all its critics. US citizen-soldier Bradley Manning was held for two years mainly in solitary confinement under abusive conditions that many equate with torture without any charges presented to a court on suspicion that he leaked documents to Wikileaks. A federal grand jury is at work in Alexandria, Virginia, concocting spy charges against Wikileaks founder Julian Assange. Obama regime official Cass Sunstein wants the 9/11 Truth movement to be infiltrated by intelligence agents and shut down.

A distinguished international attorney, Professor Francis A. Boyle of the University of Illinois, was put on the terrorist watch list because he refused an FBI/CIA request to violate the attorney-client privilege and inform on his clients.

Justin Raimondo, proprietor of the Internet news site, antiwar.com, discovered that his site was under surveillance by the FBI for suspect activities.

The CIA is prohibited from domestic spying. However, a report from the Associated Press revealed that the CIA in conjunction with the New York Police Department has been conducting a "human mapping program." According to news reports, "undercover officers known as 'rakers' have been dispatched into minority neighborhoods" to monitor "daily life in bookstores, bars, cafes and nightclubs."

Informants are used "to monitor sermons, even when there's no evidence of wrongdoing."

The police obtain informants by such means as framing Pakistani cab drivers and dropping the charges if the Pakistani agrees to infiltrate and inform on the Muslim community. The next step, of course, is to have the informer bring false charges. This illegal and unconstitutional activity is justified in the name of "preventing another 9/11."

Wired magazine reports that the FBI conducts a training program for its agents that teaches that Muslim-Americans are "violent" and "radical," even though there is no evidence that American Muslim citizens are violent and radical.[11] Americans are being turned against Muslims in a way similar to how Germans were turned against Jews. According to *Wired* magazine:

> The FBI is teaching its counterterrorism agents that 'mainstream' American Muslims are likely to be terrorist sympathizers; that the Prophet Mohammed was a 'cult leader;' and that the Islamic practice of giving charity is no more than a 'funding mechanism for combat.' At the Bureau's training ground in Quantico, Virginia, agents are shown a chart contending that the more 'devout' a Muslim, the more likely he is to be 'violent.' Those destructive tendencies cannot be reversed, an FBI instructional presentation adds: 'Any war against non-believers is justified' under Muslim law; a 'moderating process cannot happen if the Koran continues to be regarded as the word of Allah.'

Think about that for a moment. No Muslim country

has attacked the US. According to the official reports, the 9/11 hijackers were mainly Saudi Arabians and were not acting on behalf of any Muslim government. Yet, the US government has launched wars against three Muslim states—Afghanistan, Iraq, and Libya—and conducts military operations against alleged terrorists in three other Muslim states—Pakistan, Yemen, and Somalia, operations that have resulted in countless civilian deaths. General Wesley Clark has reported that Syria, Lebanon, and Iran remain on the target list.

Which is the violent state? Who is invading who? Which state is committing the war crime of unprovoked aggression?

The United States went to war against Iraq based on intentional lies about non-existent "weapons of mass destruction" and conjured up images of "mushroom clouds" from non-existent nuclear weapons programs. How does this differ from Adolf Hitler's claim that "last night Polish troops crossed the frontier and attacked Germany?"

These criminal violations of US statutory law by the US government are chosen at random among numerous similar examples. They are powerful evidence that the United States is now a police state comparable to the early stages of Stalinist Russia and Nazi Germany. This statement will seem extreme to Russians and Germans who remember the Stalin and Nazi eras. However, a police state does not require that the population of a country is put into concentration camps. Neither Stalin nor Hitler had more than a small percentage of the populations in camps. A police state is a state in which citizens do not have the protection of law and in which the government and its police agencies are not accountable to law. As the George W. Bush and Barack Obama regimes have made clear, the US government can violate its own laws, and nothing is done about it. The US government can deny its citizens their constitutional rights and nothing is done about it. The US government can announce that it has assassinated its own citizens, and nothing is done about it. The situation will worsen.

Indeed, the United States has now institutionalized the Stalinist and Gestapo practice of requiring citizens to inform on one another. In American airports, for example, there are constant announcements that people must report any suspicious activity and that everyone is subject to search at any time even after completing airport security. Homeland Security now stops traffic on the country's highways for searches.

Homeland Security instructs drivers to report "suspicious activity" by other drivers. These intrusive practices and the conditioning of citizens to spy on one another are being carried on despite the fact that there have been no terrorist events in the US since September 11, 2001 ("9/11"), except for those organized and orchestrated by the FBI in order to keep alive the fear that serves so well the growth of the "security" apparatus.*

---

* There is suspicion of the official explanation of 9/11 among some scientists, architects, engineers, pilots, and firefighters. Moreover, more than one-third of the US population is perplexed that a handful of stateless terrorists could outwit not only the CIA and FBI, but all 16 US intelligence agencies, the intelligence agencies of America's allies including Israel's Mossad, the National Security Council, NORAD, Air Traffic Control, and cause US airport security to fail four times on one morning. It is even more perplexing that such an extraordinary event could happen without the President, Congress, and the media immediately demanding an expert investigation and holding accountable those who so miserably failed in their responsibilities. Instead, the George W. Bush administration resisted for more than one year demands by 9/11 families for an investigation. The "investigation" produced a politically controlled report by the 9/11 Commission. The 9/11 Commission's co-chairmen and chief legal counsel later wrote books in which they reported that information was withheld from the commission. They described the commission as "set up to fail."

On September 11, 2011, one decade after the event that was used to turn America into a police state, three people on a flight to Detroit, Michigan, from Denver, Colorado, which landed safely with no incident, were arrested and pulled off the airliner in handcuffs.[12]

What occurred is that a woman passenger on the flight had been made paranoid by the ceaseless propaganda that Muslims, dark-skinned people, are terrorists and a threat to her life. She noticed that two dark-skinned men—who turned out to be from India—were sitting in the same row with a dark-skinned woman—who turned out to be a Jewish/Arab-American housewife in Detroit. The men frequently visited the lavatory. Remembering the "shampoo-bottled-water bomb," that came between the shoe and underwear bombs, she jumped to the conclusion that the three were terrorists and reported her finding to the airline attendant, who is required to report such "findings" of passengers to the pilots, who duly reported to higher authorities.

Whatever the procedure, when the airliner landed without any incident, because two of the three dark-skinned suspects had used the toilet facilities too often for the paranoid woman to accept as innocent, three passengers were embarrassed, abused, and taken to jail, where they were strip-searched and questioned about their nefarious intentions.

The affair turned out to be pointless. None of the arrested "suspects" had done anything, had any kind of weapon or prohibited item or improper documentation. They sat in a jail while the FBI discovered that all that had happened is that a woman made paranoid by "terrorist" reports from Fox "News" and Homeland Security had concluded that dark-skinned people who used the toilet facilities too often were terrorists.

In the event that you do not realize what this means, it means that anyone, no matter how stupid and brainwashed, can report *anyone to be a terrorist.* A fully-armed SWAT team will appear to drag the suspect from a plane, a train, a shopping center, or home, and if the latter, shoot the family dog, point automatic weapons at the family, and then justify their actions on the basis of a report from a person about whom they know nothing whatsoever. Every American is now threatened by reports stemming from jealousy, acts of revenge, or fantasy. As the massive police bureaucracy needs terrorist cases to justify its budget, there will be a growing tendency to regard reported people as guilty and to treat them as such.

As many writers who have experienced police states have made clear, once a police state is formed, the bureaucracy itself produces "suspects" and "enemies of the people." The "street sweeps" of the Stalinist era in the Soviet Union resulted from pressure on the police agency to apprehend "enemies of the people" so that the secret police themselves would not fall under Stalin's suspicion.

For now, in the early stages of the American Police State, it is still possible for innocent people to be cleared. However, too many clearances undermine the terror threat that is used to justify the abuse of citizens. The time will come when the FBI will cease to do an honest investigation that clears the accused. Everyone suspected and arrested will be declared guilty in order that the police agency proves its worth or survives suspicion from those at the top, who might be paranoid or orchestrating the system for an undeclared agenda.

That time at which accusation prevails over investigation might be close at hand. On New Year's Eve, 2011, President Obama signed the National Defense Authorization Act which contains an amendment passed with majority support of both parties (Democrats and Republicans) of both houses of Congress (House and Senate).

The amendment in effect repeals the US Constitution. This Bill of Tyranny gives the power to the US military to detain indefinitely, without presenting charges, American citizens anywhere in the world, including in the United States.

This Bill of Tyranny also repeals the Posse Comitatus Act, which has been US statutory law since 1878 and which prevents the use of the military in law enforcement against US citizens.

The executive office of the President and heads of the various security agencies wrote to Congress opposing the military detention amendment not on constitutional grounds but on the grounds that the amendment codifies in law the powers that the executive branch has achieved by assertion and with the complicity of Congress and the federal courts. The executive branch did not want its new asserted powers codified in law, because codification would reduce its flexibility and make the executive branch accountable to the law.

The executive branch said that military detention would interfere with its ability to have detainees held by the CIA in prisons that were not military prisons. Also, the Obama regime was disturbed that the implication of military detention is that detainees are prisoners of war. One of the main sponsors of the military detention amendment, Senator Carl Levin, indicated that one of the purposes of the military detention amendment was to provide some protection to detainees. Senator Levin asked and answered this question: Should somebody determined "to be a member of an enemy force who has come to this nation or is in this nation to attack us as a member of a foreign enemy, should that person be treated according to the laws of war? The answer is yes."

Detainees treated according to the laws of war have the protections of the Geneva Conventions. They cannot be tortured. The Obama regime opposed the military detention amendment to the National Defense Authorization Act, because detainees would have some rights. These rights would interfere with the regime's ability to send detainees to CIA torture prisons overseas. This is what the Obama regime means when it said that the requirement of military detention denies the regime "flexibility."

The Bush/Cheney and Obama regimes evaded the Geneva Conventions by declaring that detainees are not POWs. By classifying its prisoners as something else, the sordid government in Washington could avoid accountability for its mistreatment of detainees.

The November 17, 2011 letter to the US Senate from the Executive Office of the President says that the Obama regime does not want the authority it has under the Authorization for Use of Military Force, Public Law 107-40, to be further codified. Codification is risky says the regime: "After a decade of settled jurisprudence on detention authority, Congress must be careful not to open a whole new series of legal questions that will distract from our efforts to protect the country."[13]

In other words, the Obama regime opposed military detention not for any good reason but for a bad reason. The executive branch had achieved total discretion as to who it detains and how it treats detainees. Moreover, the lack of accountability to any law meant that no one could find out what the executive branch was doing to detainees.

Codification introduces accountability to law, and whether or not this was Congress' intention, the executive branch does not want accountability.

Obama got rid of the accountability in the amendment to the National Defense Authorization Act with signing statements, themselves unconstitutional exercises. In a word, the United States is now a lawless state. The executive branch, as long as the president declares that the country is at war, has the power of a Caesar. Congress, the alleged representatives of the people, no longer has the right to declare war or even the right to be informed when Caesar decides to take the country to war.

The Bush regime declared that the president as commander-in-chief in the "war on terror" has the prerogative to deprive US citizens of their liberty and property without due process of law. During the Obama regime, Congress attempted to codify this power in order to block the executive branch's self-transformation into a Caesar, but failed. The Obama regime added to the power of the executive the right to deprive US citizens of their lives without due process of law. Today the President of the United States sits in the Oval Office in the White House and draws up lists of people to be murdered.[14]

The degeneration of American democracy into a police state is subject matter for another book. I have provided a brief account here in order to dispel naive expectations that democracy will restore the economic prospects of citizens.

Economic Dispossession

To turn to economic dispossession, I have documented for a decade that jobs offshoring has moved to China and India and other low wage countries not merely American jobs, but also the consumer income, tax base, GDP, supply chains, and life careers associated with the jobs. (The reader might see, for example, the collection of my columns in *How the Economy Was Lost.*) I have pointed out that the result is a US unemployment rate of between one-fifth and one-fourth of the work force, a high rate that is hidden by the deceptions used in the official statistics.[15]

Until recently economists have refused to acknowledge the facts. In a subsequent section of Part Two, I examine studies of American economists, who purport to find that jobs offshoring benefits the US economy. This conclusion is so problematic that it makes me wonder if economists have been influenced by research grants, speaking fees, consultancies, and corporate board memberships. The beneficiaries of jobs offshoring are shareholders, who receive capital gains, and executives, who achieve managerial performance bonuses from the reduction in labor costs and higher profits achieved by offshoring labor.

As I have made clear in my writings over the past decade, official US statistics prove that the US has been unable for years to produce any jobs in the tradable category, whether manufacturing or professional services. In March 2011, Nobel economist Michael Spence came to the same conclusion in a paper for the Council on Foreign Relations. Spence's conclusions will be reported in subsequent sections of Part Two. Spence's analysis of the official US jobs data supports my own. The US economy has only been able to create jobs in non-tradable domestic services such as waitresses and bartenders, ambulatory health care, and retail trade. Before the real estate bubble burst, house construction was a source of jobs.

When I was Assistant Secretary of the US Treasury for Economic Policy in the Reagan administration, oil imports were the only concern in the balance of payments, and this deficit was covered by the excess of US foreign earnings abroad over payments to foreigners on their investments in the US.

In more recent times, there have been years in which the US trade deficit in manufactured goods, including high-technology goods, exceeded the oil imports. Americans no longer produce their own clothes and shoes. A significant proportion of military components is produced in foreign lands.

The high rate of US unemployment has so far proved to be immune to the stimulus of the largest federal deficits and the most aggressive monetary policy in US history. The current unemployment is unlike the post-World War II unemployment. During the second half of the 20th century, the Federal Reserve would raise interest rates and put the economy into recession in order to cool down the rate of inflation. As inflation dropped and unemployment mounted, the Federal Reserve would reverse course, cut interest rates and supply the economy with renewed growth in the money supply. Stimulative policy worked in those days, because the jobs still existed to which workers could be called back as consumer demand rose.

Today, the jobs have been moved abroad. US economic stimulus benefits China and India, but does little for US employment.

In economic theory, the rationale for the profit motive in capitalism has always been that profits indicate areas for investment and expansion, and losses indicate activities and companies that fail and go out of business. This rule is no longer observed in the US. Financial sector corporations are now "too big to fail." Consequently, bankrupt financial institutions are bailed out by taxpayer subsidies and debt monetization by the Federal Reserve. Today in America, the bigger the corporation, the less likely it will be permitted to fail regardless of the magnitude of its losses.

This procedure of rescuing failures at the expense of the population is now also the rule in the European Union. With the mega-rich subsidized by the mega-poor, is present day capitalism worse than imagined by Karl Marx?

It has not been possible for US corporations to move all manufacturing and professional service jobs, such as software engineering, offshore. Nevertheless, corporations have found another way to reduce their labor costs. The corporations tell Congress that there is a shortage of labor and that they require more foreign laborers to fill the "skill gap." The skilled workers brought in on H-1B work visas have no bargaining rights and are paid one-third less than US wages. The difference goes into corporate and shareholder profits. Modern day capitalists are loyal only to money, not to country.

Social Dispossession

Socially, America has become a third world country with a small minority of "haves" and a large majority of "have-nots." In recent years more than half of university graduates, many burdened with large student loans, are unable to find employment and have had to return to live in their childhood rooms in their parents' homes. Even many of those who found employment have to live with their parents as their salaries are insufficient to cover the rent on a residence of their own.

Millions of Americans have lost their homes and millions more are unable to make mortgage payments and are awaiting foreclosure. Americans are living in their cars and in tent cities.[16] Engineers have jobs as Wal-Mart clerks and sales clerks in department stores. Their incomes and living standards have collapsed.

Statistician John Williams (shadowstats.com) reports that real as opposed to nominal incomes continue to fall. Deflating median US income with the Consumer Price Index for urban consumers (CPI-U), Williams finds that after a decade US income levels in 2010 have not recovered their pre-2001 recession highs. Moreover, Williams reports, adjusting incomes with the traditional CPI-U measure "shows that the level of 2010 median household income is below where it was in 1969."

Studies have concluded that the richest 20 per cent of Americans control 84% of the country's wealth and that the total wealth of America's richest 400 families equals the total wealth of the bottom half of the US population, roughly 150 million people.[17] The distribution of income in the US is so heavily biased in favor of the extremely rich that the United States now has the worst distribution of income in the developed world. The US income distribution is actually worse than that of many Third World countries, falling between Uruguay and Cameroon. According to the Central Intelligence Agency, the US has a worse income distribution than Iran, Nigeria, Nicaragua, Cambodia, Thailand, Kenya, Russia, China, Senegal, Turkmenistan and Jordan.[18]

I am often asked how the American economy differs today from the years of the Reagan administration when I was a high Treasury official in charge of US economic policy. Those were pre-offshoring and pre-deregulation times, and the differences are immense. A far higher percentage of Americans were employed. The dollar was strong, not weak. Home ownership was expanding, not contracting. Commercial banks were separate from investment banks, and debt leverage was restricted. In other words, the financial system was not a casino, and corporate profits were not obtained by replacing American labor with foreign labor.

The assault on common sense rules, which governed American capitalism and made it humane, resulted from the hubris created by the triumph of capitalism over Soviet communism. The neoconservative "end of history" nonsense proclaimed that of the United States to be the only viable political-socio-economic system.[19]

This hubris caused America to over-reach and led to America's demise as a prosperous and free country.

Offshoring Displaced First World Americans

For decades the Democratic Party seemed to have a monopoly on class war with demagogy of "the rich." In the 21st century, the rich instigated class war with attacks on labor unions and middle class jobs. The ladders of upward mobility are being dismantled. America, once the land of opportunity, is now polarized between rich and poor.

The lives and careers that are being lost to the carnage of America's gratuitous wars are paralleled by the economic destruction of careers, families and communities in the U.S. Since the days of President Franklin D. Roosevelt in the 1930s, the U.S. government has sought to protect employment of its citizens. Presidents George H. W. Bush, William J. Clinton, George W. Bush and Barack Obama have turned their backs on this responsibility.

"Free trade" and "globalization" are the guises behind which class war is being conducted against the middle class by both political parties. In the 1992 US presidential campaign, billionaire Ross Perot, a political outsider and third party candidate, was the first to call national attention to the "giant sucking sound" of American jobs being offshored to foreign lands. The political establishment eliminated the threat from Perot by having the media characterize Perot as "an untested wild man." Despite the media campaign against him, Perot won 20 million votes or 19% of the popular vote.

Fourteen years later Patrick J. Buchanan, a three-time contender for the presidential nomination, wrote that NAFTA and the various so-called trade agreements are not trade agreements. They are enabling acts that empower U.S. corporations to dump their American workers, avoid Social Security taxes, health care and pension costs, and move their factories offshore to locations where labor is cheap and environmental restrictions virtually nonexistent.[20]

Perot and Buchanan were correct, and the economists were wrong. On September 20, 2011, *Manufacturing & Technology News,* citing the latest Quarterly Census of Employment and Wages, reported that during the previous ten years, the US lost 54,621 factories, and manufacturing employment fell by 5 million employees. Over the decade, the number of larger factories (those employing 1,000 or more employees) declined by 40 percent. US factories employing 500-1,000 workers declined by 44 percent; those employing between 250-500 workers declined by 37 percent, and those employing between 100-250 workers shrunk by 30 percent. These losses are net of new start-ups. Not all the losses are due to offshoring. Some are the result of business failures.

US politicians, such as Buddy Roemer, blame the collapse of US manufacturing on Chinese competition and "unfair trade practices." However, it is US corporations that move their factories abroad, thus replacing domestic production with imports. Half of US imports from China consist of the offshored production of US corporations.

The wage differential is substantial. According to the Bureau of Labor Statistics, as of 2009, average hourly take-home pay for US workers was $23.03. Social insurance expenditures add $7.90 to hourly compensation and benefits paid by employers add $2.60 per hour for a total labor compensation cost of $33.53.

In China as of 2008, total hourly labor cost was $1.36, and India's is within a few cents of this amount. Thus, a corporation that moves 1,000 jobs to China saves saves $32,000 every hour in labor cost. These savings translate into higher stock prices and executive compensation, not in lower prices for consumers who are left unemployed by the labor arbitrage.

Republican economists blame "high" US wages for the current high rate of unemployment. However, US wages are about the lowest in the developed world. They are far below hourly labor cost in Norway ($53.89), Denmark ($49.56), Belgium ($49.40), Austria ($48.04), and Germany ($46.52). The US might have the world's largest economy, but its hourly workers rank 14th on the list of the best paid.

Jobs offshoring neutralized the productivity advantages that American labor enjoyed. Working with superior capital, technology, and business organization, US workers had nothing to fear from cheap labor abroad. Americans were far more productive than Indians and Chinese, and their high productivity was reflected in high wages. American jobs and living standards were not threatened by low wages abroad or by the products that these low wages produced.

The advent of offshoring has destroyed the productivity advantage of First World labor. Offshoring makes it possible for firms using First World capital and technology to produce goods and services for the U.S. market with low wage foreign labor. The result is to separate Americans' incomes from the production of the goods and services that they consume. This new development, often called "globalization," allows cheap foreign labor to work with the same capital, technology and business know-how as U.S. workers. The foreign workers are now as productive as Americans, with the difference being that the large excess supply of labor that overhangs labor markets in China and India keeps wages low. Labor that is equally productive but paid a fraction of First World wages is a magnet for Western capital and technology.

Although a new development, offshoring is destroying entire industries, occupations and communities in the United States. The devastation of U.S. manufacturing employment was waved away and dismissed with promises that a "new economy" based on high tech knowledge jobs would take its place. Education and retraining were touted as the answer.

In testimony before the US-China Commission on September 25, 2003,[21] I explained that offshoring is the replacement of U.S. labor with foreign labor in U.S. production functions over a wide range of tradable goods and services. As the production of most tradable goods and services can be moved offshore, there are no replacement occupations for which to train except in domestic "hands on" services such as barbers, manicurists, and hospital orderlies. No country benefits from trading its professional jobs, such as engineering, for nontradable domestic service jobs.

At a Brookings Institution conference in Washington, D.C., in January 2004,[22] I predicted that if the pace of jobs offshoring and occupational destruction continued, the U.S. would be a Third World country in 20 years. Despite my regular updates on the poor performance of U.S. job growth in the 21st century, economists have insisted that offshoring is a manifestation of free trade and can only have positive benefits overall for Americans.

Reality has contradicted the glib economists. The new high-tech knowledge jobs are being outsourced abroad even faster than the old manufacturing jobs. Only a few establishment economists are beginning to see the light. Writing *in Foreign Affairs* in March/April 2006,[23] Princeton University economist and former Federal Reserve vice-chairman Alan Blinder concludes that economists who insist that offshore outsourcing is merely a routine extension of international trade are overlooking a major transformation with significant consequences. Blinder estimates that 42-56 million American service sector jobs are susceptible to offshore outsourcing. Whether all these jobs leave, U.S. salaries will be forced down by the willingness of foreigners to do the work for less.

Software engineers and information technology workers have been especially hard hit. Jobs offshoring, which began with call centers and back-office operations, is rapidly moving up the value chain. In 2005, *Business Week's* Michael Mandel compared starting salaries in 2005 with those in 2001.[24] He found a 12.7% decline in computer science pay, a 12% decline in computer engineering pay, and a 10.2% decline in electrical engineering pay.

Using the same sources as Mandel's *Business Week* article (salary data from the National Association of Colleges and Employers and Bureau of Labor Statistics data for inflation adjustment), Professor Norm Matloff at the University of California, Davis, made the same comparison for master degree graduates. He found that between 2001 and 2005 starting pay for master degrees in computer science, computer engineering and electrical engineering fell 6.6%, 13.7%, and 9.4% respectively.

Obviously, if these skills were in short supply, as corporations allege, the shortage would result in rising salaries as employers bid for scarce human resources.

On February 22, 2006, CNNMoney.com staff writer Shaheen Pasha reported that America's large financial institutions are moving "large portions of their investment banking operations abroad."[25] Offshoring is now killing American jobs in research and analytic operations, foreign exchange trades and highly complicated credit derivatives contracts. Deal-making responsibility itself may eventually move abroad. The accounting firm Deloitte Touche reported that the financial services industry will move 20 percent of its total costs base offshore by the end of 2010. As the costs are lower in India, the move will represent more than 20 percent of the business. A job on Wall Street is a declining option for bright young persons with high stress tolerance as America's last remaining advantage is outsourced abroad.

According to Norm Augustine, former CEO of Lockheed Martin, even jobs at the fast food chain, McDonald's, are on the way offshore. Augustine reports that McDonald's is experimenting with replacing error-prone order takers with a system that transmits orders via satellite to a central location and from there to the person preparing the order. The technology lets the orders be taken in India or China at costs below the US minimum wage and without the liabilities of US employees. Whether or not this works out for McDonald's, it shows that not even minimum wage domestic service jobs are safe for Americans.

American economists, some from incompetence and some from being bought-and-paid-for, describe globalization as a "win-win" development. It was supposed to work like this: The U.S. would lose market share in tradable manufactured goods and make up the job and economic loss with highly-educated knowledge workers. The win for America would be lower-priced imported manufactured goods and a white collar work force. The win for China would be manufacturing jobs that would bring economic development to that country.

It did not work out this way, as Stephen Roach, formerly a cheerleader for globalization, concluded. Roach writes that it has become apparent that job creation and real wages in the developed economies are seriously lagging their historical norms. Offshore outsourcing displaces not only manufacturing jobs, but also the "new economy" jobs in "software programming, engineering, design, and the medical profession, as well as a broad array of professionals in the legal, accounting, actuarial, consulting, and financial services industries." The real state of the U.S. job market is revealed by a *Chicago Sun-Times* report on January 26, 2006, that 25,000 people applied for 325 jobs at a new Chicago Wal-Mart.

The Evidence from the Bureau of Labor Statistics

According to the Bureau of Labor Statistics (BLS) payroll jobs data,[26] over the half-decade (January 2001-January 2006) prior to the onset of the December 2007 Great Recession, the US economy created 1,613,000 seasonally adjusted (or 1,554,000 not seasonally adjusted) net new private sector jobs and 1,012,000 seasonally adjusted (or 974,000 not seasonally adjusted) net new government jobs for a total five-year seasonally adjusted figure of 2,625,000. That is five to six million jobs short of keeping up with population growth, definitely a serious job shortfall.

The BLS payroll jobs data contradict the hype from business organizations, such as the U.S. Chamber of Commerce, that claims that offshore outsourcing is good for America. Large corporations, which have individually dismissed thousands of their U.S. employees and replaced them with foreigners, claim that jobs offshoring allows them to save money that can be used to hire more Americans. The corporations and the business organizations are very successful in placing this disinformation in the media. The lie is repeated everywhere and has become a mantra among no-think economists and politicians. However, no sign of these jobs can be found in the payroll jobs data. But there is abundant evidence of the lost American jobs.

During the first years (January 2001-January 2006) of the 21st century prior to the downturn associated with the 2008 financial crisis, the information sector of the U.S. economy lost 656,000 jobs or 17.7% of its work force. Computer systems design and related fields lost 83,500 jobs or 6.2% of its work force.[27] Clearly, jobs offshoring is not creating jobs in computers and information technology. Indeed, jobs offshoring is not even creating jobs in related fields.

In the five years between 2001 and 2006, U.S. manufacturing lost 2.9 million jobs, 17% of the manufacturing work force. The wipeout is across the board. Not a single manufacturing payroll classification created a single new job.

The declines in some manufacturing sectors have more in common with a country undergoing saturation bombing during war than with a super-economy that is "the envy of the world." Between 2001 and 2006, communications equipment lost 43% of its workforce. Semiconductors and electronic components lost 37% of its workforce. The workforce in computer and electronic products declined 30%. Electrical equipment and appliances lost 26% of its employees. The workforce in motor vehicles and parts declined 12%. Furniture and related products lost 16% of its jobs. Apparel manufacturers lost almost half of the work force. Employment in textile mills declined 43%. Paper and paper products lost one-fifth of its jobs. The work force in plastics and rubber products declined by 14%.

During the first half-decade of the 21st century, U.S. job growth was limited to four areas: education and health services, state and local government, leisure and hospitality, and financial services.

Engineering jobs in general are in decline, because the manufacturing sectors that employ engineers are in decline. During the five year period that we are examining, 2001-2006, the U.S. work force lost 1.2 million jobs in the manufacture of machinery, computers, electronics, semiconductors, communication equipment, electrical equipment, motor vehicles and transportation equipment. The BLS payroll job numbers show a total of 75,900 jobs created in all fields of architecture and engineering, including clerical personnel, over the January 2001-January 2006 period. That comes to a mere 15,180 jobs per year (including clerical workers). The fate of new university graduates cannot be very pleasant, with declining employment in the manufacturing sectors that employ engineers and a minimum of 65,000 H-1B work visas annually for foreigners plus an indeterminate number of L-1 work visas.

Not only the Bush and Obama regimes, with their claims of Iraqi "weapons of mass destruction" and "Iranian nukes," base their policies on lies, but corporations also lie about "skill shortages." Not content with moving Americans' jobs abroad, corporations want to fill the jobs remaining in America with foreigners on work visas. Business organizations allege shortages of engineers, scientists and even nurses. Business organizations have successfully used pubic relations firms and bought-and-paid-for "economic studies" to convince policymakers that American business cannot function without the subsidy provided by H-1B visas. The evidence is conclusive that the visas do not fill a "skills gap." The visas allow corporations to replace higher paid Americans with lower paid foreigners. Prior to being discharged, the American employees are first required to train their replacements. If the skills were in short supply, Americans would not be discharged when the H-1B visa holders are hired.

Keep in mind this H-1B subsidy to U.S. corporations for employing foreign workers in place of Americans as we examine the US Department of Labor's job projections over the 2004-2014 decade.

All of the occupations with the largest projected employment growth (in terms of the number of jobs) over the 2004-2014 decade are in nontradable domestic services. The top ten sources of the most jobs in "superpower" America are: retail salespersons, registered nurses, postsecondary teachers, customer service representatives, janitors and cleaners, waiters and waitresses, food preparation (includes fast food), home health aides, nursing aides, orderlies and attendants, general and operations managers. Note than none of this projected employment growth will contribute one nickel toward producing goods and services that could be exported to help close the massive U.S. trade deficit. Note, also, that few of these job classifications require a college education. The knowledge jobs that Americans have been promised for 20 years have not materialized.

Among the ten fastest growing occupations (in terms of rate of growth), seven of the ten are in health care and social assistance. The three remaining fields are: network systems and data analysis with 126,000 jobs projected or 12,600 per year; computer software engineering applications with 222,000 jobs projected or 22,200 per year, and computer software engineering systems software with 146,000 jobs projected or 14,600 per year.

Assuming these projections are realized, how many of the computer engineering and network systems jobs will go to Americans? Not many, considering the 65,000 H-1B visas each year (bills have been introduced in Congress to raise the number). The high speed Internet makes it easy for US corporations to offshore these jobs at a fraction of US salaries.

Judging from its ten-year jobs projections for the years 2004-2014, the US Department of Labor does not expect to see any significant high-tech job growth in the US. The knowledge jobs are being outsourced even more rapidly than the manufacturing jobs. The so-called "new economy" was just another hoax perpetrated on the American people.

What has been the US economy's job performance since January, 2006, and what are the latest ten-year job projections from the Department of Labor? From January 2006 to January 2011, US manufacturing lost another 2,593,000 jobs, 18% of the 2006 manufacturing work force.

For the five-year period from January 2006 through January 2011, US employment in computer and electronic products fell by 190,400 from 1,305,600 to 1,115,200, a decline of 16%. For the ten-year period from January 2001 through January 2011, US employment in computer and electronic products declined by 40%.

Employment losses show up everywhere. In the production of machinery, employment declined by 30% between January 2001 and January 2011. Employment in the manufacture of semiconductors and electronic components literally collapsed falling over the ten-year period from 714,000 to 377,500, a decline of 47%.

It is easy to bore readers with numbers, but it needs to be made clear that employment in First World jobs in the US has collapsed across the board. Employment in the manufacture of electrical equipment and appliances during the first decade of the 21st century declined by 37%. US employment in the manufacture of motor vehicles and parts declined by 44%. Employment in textile mills fell by 66%. Employment in the manufacture of clothing fell by 65%. Employment in the chemical industry fell by 21%.

Employment even fell by 1% in financial activities, supposedly the backbone of the "new economy."

In what areas did US employment grow during the first decade of the 21st century? In January 2011 there were 1,132,300 more waitresses and bartenders than in January 2001, a gain of 14%. Employment in health care and social assistance increased by 3,686,300, a gain of 29%. Ambulatory health care services accounted for 1,666,300 of these jobs, or 45%. Government employment grew by 1,391,000. As of January 2011 total government employment in the US was 22,226,000, almost twice the number of Americans (11,618,000) employed in manufacturing.

The evidence is conclusive, "globalism" or jobs offshoring has given US employment a Third World complexion with jobs available only in government and nontradable domestic services.

The US Bureau of Labor Statistics' projections for US job growth between 2008 and 2018 reinforces this conclusion. The BLS projects a 3.5% decline in employment in production occupations such as manufacturing over the coming years. Job growth is projected only for services: nurses, nursing aides, health aides, orderlies, attendants, customer service representatives, food preparation and serving, retail salespersons, office clerks, managers of office and administrative support workers, security guards, waiters and waitresses, truck drivers. The few occupations projected to add jobs that require university education are accountants, teachers, computer software engineers, network systems and data communications, and management analysts.[28] Again, because of jobs offshoring and H-1B visas there is no guarantee that software engineering and IT jobs will go to Americans.

The BLS projects that of the thirty occupations with the largest employment growth only seven require university degrees. The BLS projects jobs for university graduates to total 1,434,000 over the decade of 2008-2018. This figure is only 60% of the number of university graduates projected by the National Center for Education Statistics *for the academic year 2011-2012 alone.*[29]

In other words, over the 2008-2018 decade, there will be many times more US university graduates than there will be new jobs.

The National Center for Education Statistics projects that the academic year 2011-2012 will produce 1,570,000 bachelor degrees, 671,000 master's degrees, 98,500 professional degrees (medical doctors, dentists, lawyers), and 52,700 Ph.D. degrees, for a total of 2,392,200. If the 731,000 two-year Associate Degrees (for example, the qualification for a registered nurse) are included, US colleges and universities are projected to graduate 3,123,200 people from the 2011-2012 academic year.

Where are these graduates going to find employment? To see the extent of the problem, consider the projection by the National Center for Education Statistics that from the academic year 2007-2008 through the academic year 2013-2014, a seven-year period, there will be a total of 16,309,000 university graduates with bachelor, master, Ph.D. and professional degrees. If we include the approximately 5,000,000 associate degrees, we have a 7-year graduate total of more than 21,000,000 for which the BLS projects employment prospects of 143,400 per year for university graduates and 58,200 per year for registered nurses with Associate Degrees.

Many graduates of US universities are foreigners. I have been unable to find numbers for foreign graduates of US universities by year and am unable to learn what percentage of these graduates return to their home countries. I will make an estimate based on my having attended recent graduation ceremonies at Stanford University, Georgia Tech, and the University of Missouri. I would estimate that one-third of the graduates were not US citizens. Let's raise that estimate to one-half, and let's assume that all foreign graduates return to their home countries. That leaves 8 million American US university graduates over a 7-year period chasing 1,434,000 jobs over a 10-year period.

Retirements also provide job opportunities for new graduates. To compute the extent of the surplus of university graduates, we would have to have the retirement rate and to know how many retirees are replaced by new hires. Nevertheless, considering the large number of graduates compared to the small number of new jobs that require a university education, it is difficult to see a future for education in America.

According to experts, the US economy must create between 130,000 and 150,000 new jobs each month just to stay even with population growth. To reduce the high rate of unemployment requires higher job growth. If we use the lower figure of 130,000, 1,560,000 new jobs are needed per year to keep unemployment from rising. Over a ten year period 15,600,000 jobs would be required. The US economy has not come close to generating the number of jobs required by population growth. The Bureau of Labor Statistics reports that over the ten-year period January 2001 to January 2011, the US economy lost 2,141,000 jobs. That leaves a deficit of 17,741,000 jobs.[30]

The "new economy's" knowledge jobs are nowhere to be found. Merely three occupations which only require short or medium term on-the-job-training—home health aides, customer service representatives, and food preparation—are projected to add almost as many jobs as the occupations that require a university education. Of the top ten occupational classifications with the largest projected job growth, only accountants and auditors (number 8) and postsecondary teachers (number 10) require university degrees.

This is the "new economy" bequeathed by globalism that takes the place of the old manufacturing/industrial economy. The promised "knowledge jobs" are nowhere in the picture. America has become a "superpower" with a Third World work force employed in lowly paid domestic services.

While jobs offshoring destroyed US employment and consumer income growth, government, corporations and their shills among economists and in the media produced a constant flow of assurances that "globalism" was good for America. During the George W. Bush regime, the US Department of Commerce spent $335,000 to study the impact of the offshoring of US high-tech jobs, but refused to release the study. Republican political appointees reduced the 200-page report to 12 pages of public relations hype and refused to allow the Technology Administration experts who wrote the report to testify before Congress.

Democrats on the House Science Committee were unable to pry the study out of the hands of Commerce Secretary Carlos Gutierrez. On March 29, 2006, Republicans on the House Science Committee voted down a resolution (H.Res. 717) designed to force the Commerce Department to release the study to Congress. Obviously, the facts did not fit the Bush regime's globalization hype.

The BLS payroll data that we have examined tracks employment by industry classification. This is not the same thing as occupational classification. For example, companies in almost every industry and area of business employ people in computer-related occupations. A study (2004) from the Association for Computing Machinery claims: "Despite all the publicity in the United States about jobs being lost to India and China, the size of the IT employment market in the United States today is higher than it was at the height of the dot.com boom. Information technology appears as though it will be a growth area at least for the coming decade."

We can check this claim by turning to the November 2004 BLS Occupational Employment Statistics.. We will look at "computer and mathematical employment" and "architecture and engineering employment."

Computer and mathematical employment includes such fields as "software engineers applications," "software engineers systems software," "computer programmers," "network systems and data communications," and "mathematicians." Has this occupation been a source of job growth?

In November of 2000 this occupation employed 2,932,810 people . In November of 2004, this occupation employed 2,932,790, or 20 people fewer. Stagnant employment is not "high growth."[31]

Architecture and engineering employment includes all the architecture and engineering fields except software engineering. The total employment of architects and engineers in the U.S. declined by 120,700 between November 1999 and November 2004. Whatever the year used as the base employment declined. For example, employment declined by 189,940 between November 2000 and November 2004, and by 103,390 between November 2001 and November 2004.

Clearly, engineering and computer-related employment in the US did not grow during the period as claimed by the Association of Computing Machinery. Moreover, with a half million foreigners in the U.S. on work visas, the overall employment numbers do not represent employment of Americans.

American employees have been abandoned by American corporations and by their representatives in Congress. America remains a land of opportunity—but for foreigners—not for the native born. A country whose work force is concentrated in domestic nontradable services has no need for scientists and engineers and no need for universities. Even the projected jobs in nursing and school teachers can be filled by foreigners on H-1B visas.

In the U.S. the myth has been firmly established that the jobs that have been moved offshore are being replaced with better jobs. There is no sign of these jobs in the payroll jobs data or in the occupational employment statistics. When a country loses entry level jobs, it has no one to promote to senior level jobs. When manufacturing leaves, so does engineering, design, research and development, and innovation itself.

On February 16, 2006, *The New York Times* reported on a new study presented to the National Academies that concludes that job offshoring is climbing the skills ladder. A survey of 200 multinational corporations representing 15 industries in the U.S. and Europe found that 38 percent planned to change substantially the worldwide distribution of their research and development work, sending it to India and China. According to *The New York Times*, "More companies in the survey said they planned to decrease research and development employment in the United States and Europe than planned to increase employment."[32]

The study and the discussion it provoked came to untenable remedies. Many believe that a primary reason for the shift of R&D to India and China is the erosion of scientific prowess in the U.S. due to lack of math and science proficiency of American students and their reluctance to pursue careers in science and engineering. This belief begs the question why students would chase after careers that are being outsourced abroad.

No one seems to understand that research, development, design, and innovation take place in countries *where things are made*. The loss of manufacturing means ultimately the loss of engineering and science. The newest plants embody the latest technology. If these plants are abroad, that is where the cutting edge resides.

When a country gives up producing tradable goods, it gives up the occupations associated with manufacturing. Engineering and R&D depart with the manufacturing. It is impossible to innovate independently of the manufacturing and R&D base. Innovation is based on state-of-the-art knowledge of what is being done, and if the doing is done elsewhere, the innovator will be at a disadvantage.

Offshoring is causing dire problems for the United States. I have suggested that one necessary reform is to break the connection between CEO pay and short-run profit performance. As long as CEOs can become rich in a few years by dumping their U.S. workforce, the trade deficit will continue to rise, and more college graduates will be employed as waitresses and bartenders.

The short-run time horizon of U.S. management endangers the long-term viability of U.S. firms. This short-run time horizon is the result of a "reform" that sought to give investors the most up-to-date financial information by requiring quarterly reporting. The reformers did not consider the unintended consequences, which was to focus Wall Street, corporate executives, and boards of directors on short-run performance.

Economists need to inject some realism into their dogmas. The U.S. economy did not develop on the basis of free trade. If the costs that free traders attribute to trade protection are real, the costs did not prevent America's economic rise. Indeed, much historical research concludes that trade protection was the reason for America's rise as an industrial and manufacturing power.[33] Frank William Taussig in his book, *The Tariff History of the United States,*[34] documents that trade protection, not free trade, was US economic policy in the 19th century. Taussig argues that although the US had extensive trade protection, tariffs were not the main cause of the rise of the US as a manufacturing country and that both opponents and advocates of protective duties exaggerate their effects.

Much American economic thinking is grounded in the fact of America's past success. Many economists take it for granted that as long as the U.S. has free markets, it will continue to be successful. However, much of America's success is due to World War I and World War II, which bankrupted rivals and destroyed their industrial capacity. It was easy for the United States to dominate world trade after

World War II, because America was the only country with an intact manufacturing economy and the US dollar replaced the British pound as world reserve currency.

Many economists dismiss the problems with which offshoring confronts developed economies with the argument that it is just a question of wage equilibration. As wages rise in China and India, the labor cost differential will disappear, and wages will be the same everywhere. This argument overlooks the lengthy period required for the hundreds of millions of workers, who overhang labor markets in India and China, to be absorbed into the workforce. During this time, hardships in currently high-wage countries would be severe. Moreover, once the wage adjustment is complete, the new developed countries would have the upper hand. Would they give up their competitive and strategic advantages?

The Myth of Benevolent Globalism

The United States is the first country in modern history to destroy the prospects and living standards of its labor force in order to enrich the top 1% of the income distribution. Once a land of opportunity, America is being polarized by globalism into rich and poor. The denial of this reality has become an art form for economists.

For example, Matthew J. Slaughter, a member of President George W. Bush's Council of Economic Advisers, wrote: "For every one job that U.S. multinationals created abroad in their foreign affiliates, they created nearly two U.S. jobs in their parent operations." In other words, Slaughter claims that offshoring is creating more American jobs than foreign ones.

Slaughter did not arrive at this conclusion by consulting the BLS payroll jobs data or the BLS Occupational Employment Statistics. Instead, Slaughter measured the growth of U.S. multinational employment and failed to take into account the reasons for the increase in multinational employment. Multinationals acquired many existing smaller firms, thus raising multinational employment but not overall employment, and many U.S. firms established foreign operations for the first time and thereby became multinationals, thus adding their existing employment to multinational employment.

Economists find many ways to obscure the facts. For example, Matthew Spiegleman, a Conference Board economist, claimed that manufacturing jobs are only slightly higher paid than domestic service jobs, so there is no meaningful loss in income to Americans from offshoring. He reached this conclusion by comparing only hourly pay and leaving out the longer manufacturing work week and the associated benefits, such as health care and pensions that are part of renumeration to full-time manufacturing workers.

At a November 2006 press conference in Washington, D.C., Harvard University professor Michael Porter introduced a report from the Council on Competitiveness titled "Competitiveness Index: Where America Stands." Porter, a principal author of the report, said that the report showed that Americans were benefitting from globalism.

Porter's claims were inconsistent with empirical data, a fact that I pointed out at the time. Nevertheless, the Council on Competitiveness defended its report, and it became part of the stack of reports that have been used to convince Americans that they are benefitting from what is destroying them.

The competitiveness report boasts that the United States "leads all major economies in GDP per capita;" that "household wealth grew strongly, supported by gains in real estate and stocks;" and that "poverty rates improved for all groups over the past two decades."

By covering a 20-year period, the report was able to soften the economic deterioration from globalism with stronger performance from earlier periods. As globalism becomes more pronounced, Porter's report shows that the U.S. economy performs less well. Indeed, the report acknowledges under-performance in critical areas. The gains that Porter finds over 20 years have their roots in the earlier period in President Reagan's supply-side policy. They are not gains from jobs offshoring.

When Porter's report was released, U.S. job creation in the 21st century was below past performance. Debt payments of Americans as a percent of their disposable incomes were rising while the savings rate had collapsed into dis-saving. Poverty rates had turned back up in the 21st century when the impact of globalism on Americans has been most pronounced.

The report mentions many times that the United States is the driver of global growth without emphasizing that U.S. growth is debt-driven. In 2006 both the U.S. government and U.S. consumers were accumulating debt at a rapid pace. At the time of Porter's report, debt-driven consumption was exceeding U.S. output by a sum in excess of $800 billion annually. Trade and current account deficits were threatening the dollar's role as reserve currency. The competitiveness report makes these negatives sound like America is leading the world by driving economic growth.

The report claims, as do many economists, that the "U.S.A. attracts most foreign direct investment," and that "the United States remains a magnet for global investment" because of "America's high levels of productivity, strong growth and unparalleled consumer market." This claim fails to differentiate between investment in new plant and equipment and investment in existing assets.

Porter's report suggests that foreign direct investment in the U.S. consists of new plant and equipment, and thus is creating jobs for Americans. However, reports from the Bureau of Economic Analysis, U.S. Department of Commerce, show that the statistical evidence is clear that foreign direct investment in the United States consists almost entirely of foreign acquisitions of existing U.S. companies. Foreign direct investment is merely the counterpart of the huge American trade and current account deficits. America pays for its over-consumption in dollars which foreigners use to buy up existing U.S. businesses.

For example, the BEA's June, 2009, report, "Foreign Direct Investment in the United States" by Thomas Anderson, divides foreign direct investment into its two components, acquisitions of existing businesses and establishment of new businesses, for the years 1992-2008. In 1992, new businesses comprised 30.8% of foreign direct investment in the U.S., and acquisitions of existing businesses comprised 69.2%. In 1997, the percentages were 12.9 and 87.1 respectively. In 2000, the percentages were 3.8 and 96.2. In 2007, the percentages were 11.2 and 88.8. In 2008, the percentages were 6.7 and 93.2.[35]

Offshoring increases the US trade deficit by the amount of goods and services produced offshore for US markets. The trade deficit is financed by turning over ownership of US companies to foreigners, and the incomes from these acquired businesses worsen the current account.

The Council on Competitiveness report is also mistaken in its assessment of U.S. productivity growth. Economists maintain that labor is paid according to its productivity, and historically this has been the case in the United States. The correlation began to break down with the advent of offshoring to the Asian Tigers and deteriorated further with the advent of offshoring of manufacturing and service jobs to China and India. The historical correlation between productivity and wages has been further eroded by the importation into the United States of cheap foreign skilled labor on work visas. Many Americans have been forced to train their foreign replacements, essentially indentured servants, who work for one-third less pay. The result is a widening divergence of labor productivity from real compensation as Bureau of Labor Statistics, U.S. Department of Labor, reports show.

For the years 1947-73, the growth in real hourly compensation was 93% of labor productivity growth, dropping to 82% for the years 1973-79. For the last decade of the 20th century, labor's compensation had fallen to 71% of productivity growth. During the first decade of the 21st century, labor's share plummeted to 44%.[36]

The greatest failure in the competitiveness report is the absence of mention of the labor arbitrage and its consequences when U.S. firms offshore their production for U.S. markets. This practice translates into direct job loss and direct tax base loss, and it transforms domestic output into imports. Offshoring is capital and technology chasing absolute advantage abroad. Offshoring cannot be justified as free trade based on resources finding their comparative advantage in the domestic economy.

It is this replacement of the US workforce by foreign workers that explains the extraordinary rise in CEO compensation and the flow of the income and wealth gains to the few people at the top. By offshoring their workforces, CEOs cut their costs and make or exceed their earnings forecasts, thus receiving bonuses that are many multiples of their salaries. Shareholders benefit from the rise in share prices. When plants are closed and jobs are offshored, American employees lose their livelihoods, but managements and shareholders prosper. Offshoring is causing an extraordinary increase in American income inequality.

The 2006 Council on Competitiveness report acknowledges that "for the first time in history, emerging economies, such as China, are loaning enormous amounts of money to the world's richest country." Historically, it was rich countries that lent to underdeveloped countries.

China's loans to the United States are a form of forced lending. China receives dollars from America's dependency on imports of manufactured and advanced technology products made in China by US and Chinese firms. China uses the dollars to purchase existing U.S. equity assets and to lend the dollars back to the United States by purchasing Treasury debt. With China's currency pegged to the dollar, China cannot dump the dollars into foreign exchange markets without initiating a run on the dollar and complaints that China is increasing its competitive advantage over the rest of the world by driving down the US dollar in order to devalue its own currency.

When I was Assistant Secretary of the U.S. Treasury in the early 1980s, U.S. foreign assets exceeded foreign-owned assets in the United States. By 2005 this had changed dramatically, with foreigners owning $2.7 trillion more of the U.S. than the U.S. owns abroad. For the first time since the United States was a developing country 90 years ago, the US is paying more to foreign creditors than it is receiving from its investments abroad.

Porter's report downplays the trade and current account deficits on the grounds that "foreign affiliate sales" do not count against the trade deficit and "intra-firm trade" is a significant proportion of the trade deficit and "is due to trade within American companies."

"Intra-firm trade" is simply a company's offshored production produced in its offshore plants, and "foreign affiliate sales" is simply a company's overseas revenues from its production in foreign countries with foreign labor.

Perhaps Porter is arguing that the output of an American subsidiary in Germany, for example, should be considered part of U.S. GDP. Such accounting would result in a magical increase in U.S. GDP and drop in German GDP. If success is defined in terms of the country in which the ownership of the profits of global firms resides, then a country can be successful with its labor force unemployed.

The competitiveness report owes much of its failure to an abstraction— "the global labor supply." There is no global labor market that equilibrates wages in the different countries. There are only national labor markets in which wages reflect cost of living and labor supply.

For example, in China, the cost of living is low, and excess supplies of labor suppress manufacturing wages below labor's contribution to output. In the United States, the cost of living and debt levels are high, and the labor market (except for those parts hardest hit by offshoring) is not confronted with large excess supplies of labor. The excess supply of labor in China has been estimated to equal the population of the US. It is possible for a US-based firm to hire someone living in China or India to deliver services over the Internet at a fraction of the cost of hiring an American employee. Alternatively, foreigners can be brought in on work visas to replace American employees. Manufacturing plants can be moved abroad where excess supplies of labor keep wages low. These are all examples of capital seeking absolute advantage in lowest factor cost ("factor" refers to factor of production, in this case labor).

Porter's report claims that the future of U.S. competitiveness depends on education. Although the United States has 17 of the world's top 20 research universities, Porter sees education as the number-one weakness of the U.S. economic system. The report envisions a high-wage service economy based on imagination and ingenuity. Here the competitiveness report becomes self-delusion. Porter does not comprehend that all tradable services can be offshored.

As we have seen, in the 21st century, the U.S. economy has been able to create net new jobs *only* in non-tradable domestic services. The vast majority of jobs in the BLS ten-year jobs projections do not require a college education. The problem in 21st century America is not a lack of educated people, but a lack of jobs for educated people.

Many American software engineers, IT professionals, and scientists have been forced by jobs offshoring to abandon their professions. The November 6, 2006, issue of *Chemical & Engineering News* reports that "the percentage of American Chemical Society member chemists in the domestic workforce who did not have full-time jobs as of March of this year was 8.7 percent." There is no reason for Americans to pursue education in science and technology when career opportunities in those fields are declining due to offshoring.

Porter says the future for America cannot be found in manufacturing or tradable goods, but only in what he says are high-wage service skills in "expert thinking" and "complex communication." Porter does not identify these jobs. As we have seen, no sign of them can be found in the BLS jobs data.

Even economists who realize that there is a problem cannot get their minds around it. For example, disturbed by evidence that investment by US industry in research and development was declining, the National Association of Manufacturers commissioned a report, "US Manufacturing Innovation at Risk," by economists Joel Popkin and Kathryn Kobe. In the report, released in February 2006, the economists find that U.S. industry's investment in research and development is not languishing after all. It just appears to be languishing, because it is rapidly being shifted overseas:

"Funds provided for foreign-performed R&D have grown by almost 73 percent between 1999 and 2003, with a 36 percent increase in the number of firms funding foreign R&D."

US industry is still investing in R&D after all; it is just not hiring Americans to do the research and development. U.S. manufacturers still make things, only less and less in America with American labor. U.S. manufacturers still hire engineers, only they are foreign ones, not American ones.

Everything is fine for U.S. manufacturers. It is their former American work force that is languishing. As these Americans, who are experiencing declining incomes, happen to be customers for U.S. manufacturers, U.S. brand names will gradually lose their U.S. market. U.S. household median income has been falling for years. Consumer demand has been kept alive by consumers' spending their savings and home equity and going deeper into debt. As millions of Americans together with Greece, Spain, and Italy discovered, it is not possible for debt to forever rise faster than income.

Princeton University economist Alan Blinder, my former *Business Week* colleague and former vice chairman of the Federal Reserve, also has difficulty acknowledging the implications of his conclusions. Blinder writes that "we have so far barely seen the tip of the offshoring iceberg, the eventual dimensions of which may be staggering".[37] Blinder has estimated that as many as 50 million jobs in tradable services are at risk of being offshored to lower-paid foreigners.

Like Porter and others, Blinder says that America's future lies in high-tech service jobs such as those delivering "creativity and imagination." Blinder understands that the education solution might be a pipe dream as such abilities "are notoriously difficult to teach in schools." Blinder also understands that "it is hard to imagine that truly creative positions will ever constitute anything close to the majority of jobs." Blinder asks: "What will everyone else do?"

Blinder understands that the wage differentials between the United States and India means that Americans will find employment only in services that are not deliverable electronically, such as janitors and crane operators. These hands-on service jobs do "not correspond to traditional distinctions between jobs that require high levels of education and jobs that do not."

Blinder's prediction of the future of American employment is in line with my own and that of the Bureau of Labor Statistics. But Blinder warns against saving US jobs with protectionist measures, and he does not realize the implication of these trends on the U.S. trade deficit. A country whose workforce is employed in domestic non-tradable services is a Third World country with little to export. How will the United States pay for its heavy dependence on imports of manufactured goods and energy?

As long as the dollar retains its reserve currency role, Americans can continue to hand over paper for real goods and services. But how long can the United States retain the reserve currency role when its economy does not make things to export, when its work force is employed in domestic services, and when its foreign creditors own its assets?

For developed economies, offshoring is a reversal of the development process. As offshoring progresses, the domestic economy becomes less developed, and there is less demand for university education. Economists cannot speak the obvious truth, because they confuse jobs offshoring with free trade, when in fact offshoring is a process of deindustrialization. The reformulation of trade theory achieved by Ralph Gomory and William Baumol was published by MIT Press six years prior to Porter's report, but there is no mention of this seminal work in Porter's report. Just as Porter's report ignored the empirical evidence, it ignored the reformulation of trade theory.

Why are economists content with free trade policy that rests in fantastic error?

Perhaps the answer is that the corruption of the outside world has found its way into universities. Today, universities look upon "name" professors as rainmakers who bring in funds from well-heeled interest groups. Increasingly, research and reports serve the interests that finance them and not the truth. Money rules, and professors who bring money to universities find it increasingly difficult to avoid serving the agendas of donors. The same is true of think-tanks.

Dissenters from the Myth of Benevolent Globalism

Economists other than myself have warned that it is impossible for a country to remain prosperous when its economy is moved offshore. Herman Daly, Charles McMillion, and Ralph Gomory, for example, all saw the ruinous implications of offshoring. However, it was two billionaire businessmen, Roger Milliken and Sir James Goldsmith, who first warned that offshoring would destroy the position of First World labor.

Textile magnate Roger Milliken spent his time on Capitol Hill, not on yachts with Playboy centerfolds, trying to make Washington aware that America was losing its economy. Sir James Goldsmith made his fortune by correcting the mistakes of incompetent corporate CEOs by taking over companies and putting the assets to better use. Sir James spent his last years warning of the perils both of globalism and of merging the sovereignties of European countries and the UK into the EU.

Sir James's book, *The Trap*, was published as long ago as 1993. His book, *The Response*, in which he replied to the free trade ideologues in the financial press and academia who denigrated his warning, was published in 1995. In 1994

Sir James gave a speech to the U.S. Senate warning of the perils of globalism.

Both billionaires predicted that the working and middle classes in the United States and Europe would be ruined by the greed of Wall Street and corporations. Corporate earnings would be boosted by replacing domestic work forces with foreign labor, which could be paid a fraction of labor's contribution to output as a result of the foreign country's low living standard and large excess supply of labor. Anytime there is an excess supply of labor, or the ability of corporations to pay labor less than its worth, the corporations bank the difference. Share prices rise, and Wall Street and shareholders are happy.

In March, 2011, a Nobel prize-winning economist, Michael Spence, assisted by Sandile Hlatshwayo, a researcher at New York University, lent their authority to the 20th century conclusions of Milliken and Goldsmith and to those of myself, McMillion, Daly, and Gomory. Their research report, "The Evolving Structure of the American Economy and the Employment Challenge, was published by the Council on Foreign Relations, an organization of the American Establishment.[38]

Here is what Spence and Hlatshwayo report:

This paper examines the evolving structure of the American economy, specifically, the trends in employment, value added, and value added per employee from 1990 to 2008. These trends are closely connected with complementary trends in the size and structure of the global economy, particularly in the major emerging economies. Employing historical time series data from the Bureau of

Labor Statistics and the Bureau of Economic Analysis, U.S. industries are separated into internationally tradable and non-tradable components, allowing for employment and value-added trends at both the industry and the aggregate level to be examined. Value added grew across the economy, but almost all of the incremental employment increase of 27.3 million jobs was on the non-tradable side. On the non-tradable side, government and health care are the largest employers and provided the largest increments (an additional 10.4 million jobs) over the past two decades. There are obvious questions about whether those trends can continue; without fast job creation in the non-tradable sector, the United States would already have faced a major employment challenge.

The trends in value added per employee are consistent with the adverse movements in the distribution of U.S. income over the past 20 years, particularly the subdued income growth in the middle of the income range. The tradable side of the economy is shifting up the value-added chain with lower and middle components of these chains moving abroad, especially to the rapidly growing emerging markets. The latter themselves are moving rapidly up the value-added chains, and higher-paying jobs may therefore leave the United States, following the migration pattern of lower-paying ones. The evolution of the U.S. economy supports the notion of there being a long-term structural challenge with respect to the quantity and quality of employment opportunities in the United States. A related set of challenges concerns the income distribution; almost all incremental employment has occurred in the non-tradable sector, which has experienced much slower growth in value added per employee. Because that number is highly correlated with income, it goes a long way to explain the stagnation of wages across large segments of the workforce.

What is Spence telling us? Spence is careful not to say that globalism is the intentional result of enhancing capital's profits at the expense of labor's wages, but he does acknowledge that that is its effect and that globalism or jobs offshoring has the costs that Daly, Gomory, McMillion, Milliken, Goldsmith and I have pointed out. Spence uses the same data that I have provided that proves that during the era of globalism the U.S. economy has created new jobs only in nontradable services that cannot be offshored or be produced in locations distant from the market for the services. For example, the services of barbers, waitresses, bar tenders and hospital workers, unlike those of software engineers, cannot be exported. They can only be sold locally in the location where they are provided.

Tradable jobs are jobs that produce goods and services that can be exported and thus can be produced in locations distant from their market. Tradable jobs result in higher value-added and, thereby, higher pay than most non-tradable jobs.

When a country's tradable goods and services are converted by offshoring into its imports, the country's employment changes to low productivity domestic service jobs. These domestic service jobs, except for dentists, lawyers, teachers and medical doctors do not require a university education. Yet, America has thousands of universities and colleges, and the government endlessly repeats the mantra that "education is the answer."

My hat is off to Michael Spence, a Nobel economist who has made it clear that the "New Economy" is the offshored economy.

The Decimated American Economy

Globalism is a conspiracy against First World jobs. It is the process by which capital extracts surplus and appropriates the earnings of labor. By moving offshore the production of goods and services for the home market, corporations benefit from labor arbitrage. Because of large excess supplies of labor, especially in China and India, First World corporations can hire labor at wages below the value of labor's contribution to output, thus raising the earnings of capital.

As globalism is also a conspiracy against Third World agricultural communities, which are turned into monocultures that serve global capital, some readers might object to my emphasis on globalism's harmful effects on the US economy. Why, they might ask, am I concerned only with the rich Americans and not with the poor in Africa, Latin America and Asia?

Others have documented the damage done by globalism to these countries. I refer the reader in particular to Michel Chossudovsky, *The Globalization of Poverty.* The assumption has been that these countries are plundered for the benefit of the West. But unless the West is defined as a few large corporations and banks, this is not the case. There is no better way to demonstrate that globalism is not in the world's interest than to show that it has damaged the economy of the country most expected to benefit—the hegemonic superpower, the United States of America.

Unemployment

The US economy has been unable to generate full employment for a decade. As of August 2011, there were 6.7 million fewer jobs than in January 2008, the employment peak of the 21st century prior to the financial crisis. There were 2.1 million fewer jobs in January 2011 than in January 2001. After ten years of immigration and population growth, there are fewer US jobs than a decade ago.

The economy's inability to generate jobs has left Americans with a high rate of unemployment. The 7.5% unemployment rate as of April 2013 (known as U.3) used by the financial press is misleading. It does not include discouraged workers and workers in part-time jobs who cannot find full-time jobs. The Bureau of Labor Statistics knows that the U.3 measure of unemployment is unrealistic and provides another measure, U.6, which includes short-term discouraged workers. This measure of unemployment was 13.9% in April 2013, but even this measure understates the unemployment. In 1994 the US government ceased to include long-term unemployment as part of the labor force in order to minimize the rate of unemployment. Statistician John Williams (shadowstats.com) continues to estimate long-term unemployment. He adds the number of long-term unemployed to the U.6 measure, which results in an unemployment rate of 23%. A country with between one-fifth and one-fourth of its labor force out of work is certainly not benefiting from globalism or from financial deregulation.

Inflation

During the Clinton regime the consumer price index (the measure of inflation) ceased to be based on a fixed basket of goods that measured a constant standard of living. The principle of substitution was introduced. The assumption is that if the price of an item rises, people switch to a less expensive substitute. In other words, the new consumer price index (CPI) shows lower inflation by measuring a lower standard of living. Some people have responded to the new measure by joking that when home heating costs rise, consumers switch to sweaters and heavy coats, thus eliminating the rising cost of energy from the measure of inflation.

The rate of inflation is also lowered by redefining numerous price increases as quality improvements. John Williams continues to measure inflation by the official government methodology prior to the changes that result in an understated measure of inflation. Using the original methodology, Williams finds the US inflation rate as of April 2013 to be 8.7%, which is 8.2 times the government's official rate of 1.06%.

Note that whichever measure of inflation is used, real interest rates on US debt instruments are negative. By suppressing interest rates, the Federal Reserve is reducing consumer purchasing power and living standards and forcing retired people to spend their capital as their saving accounts produce no income.

Gross Domestic Product (GDP)

Gross Domestic Product is a measure that is adjusted for inflation in order to know real output instead of a measure inflated by price increases. The "recovery" from the US recession associated with the real estate collapse and financial crisis was achieved by deflating GDP with an understated measure of inflation. When inflation as measured by previous methodology is used, US GDP growth shows no recovery.

US Wealth and Income Distribution

As we have seen, the income gains from globalism have flowed to the mega-rich. Everyone else has been dispossessed. Income distribution is calculated from the Lorenz curve and presented as a Gini index. According to the Central Intelligence Agency (CIA), the US has a Gini index of 45, which places the US among the countries with the worst income distribution. Namibia has the worst income distribution with a Gini index of 70.7, and Sweden has the most equal income distribution with a Gini index of 23.[39]

In the US the distribution and control over wealth is even worse than the income distribution. In the 1960s, despite President John F. Kennedy's reduction in marginal tax rates, which President Ronald Reagan's tax rate reduction paralleled, the top one percent received ten percent of income gains, and the bottom ninety percent received sixty-five percent of the income gains.

During the first decade of the 21st century, this distribution reversed. The top one percent received sixty-five percent of the income gains, and the bottom ninety percent received twelve percent. Globalism was a powerful contributor to this reversal, because it transformed Americans' wages and salaries into capital gains and executive bonuses.

In America poor people are now abundant. In 313 counties of American states, life expectancy for women has declined over the past 20 years. Six million more Americans have fallen into poverty since 2004. In September 2011 the US Census Bureau released a survey showing that one in six Americans now live in poverty, a new high.[40] Fifty million Americans rely on food stamps, a government food program for the poor.

The Census Bureau also reported that real median household incomes dropped 2.3 percent in 2010 from 2009, and that the top twenty percent of the income distribution controls eighty-four percent of US wealth. The distribution of wealth in the US is so highly concentrated that the 400 richest US families, all of whom are billionaires, have the same net worth as the fifty percent less well-off Americans. When 400 people have the same wealth as 150,000,000, clearly things are out of balance.

Lies That Killed the American Dream:
The Science and Technology Skills Shortage Myth

Corporations have not been content only to offshore American jobs. Business leaders are also replacing Americans with foreigners in those jobs that corporations find convenient to retain in the US. Business leaders claim that they cannot find enough Americans with science and engineering degrees to fill the jobs. Corporation executives have been successful in lobbying Congress for work visas for foreigners, who are employed in place of Americans at substantially lower costs in violation of the rules governing the work visa programs.

The two largest programs are the H-1B visas for skills in short supply and L-1 visas that allow multinational companies to bring foreign employees to the US for "training." The legislation creating the H-1B visas specifies that visas are not to be used for the replacement of US workers and that foreigners on the visas should be paid the same as American workers. Corporations easily evade these restrictions. They hire law firms to advertise job openings in ways that disqualify Americans. Moreover, H-1B visas are becoming the property of businesses that supply foreign employees to US corporations on a contract basis. The corporations hire the businesses to supply the personnel; they do not hire the individuals themselves, which has the advantage of further reducing the cost.

In June 2007, a revealing marketing video from the law firm, Cohen & Grigsby appeared on the Internet. The video demonstrated the law firm's techniques for getting around US law governing work visas in order to enable corporate clients to replace their American employees with foreigners who work for less. The law firm's marketing manager, Lawrence Lebowitz, is frank with interested clients: *"our goal is clearly not to find a qualified and interested US worker."*

If an American somehow survives the weeding out process, the law firm advises its corporate clients to "have the manager of that specific position step in and go through the whole process to find a legal basis to disqualify him for this position—in most cases there doesn't seem to be a problem."

No problem for the employer he means, only for the expensively educated American university graduate who is displaced by a foreigner imported on a work visa justified by a nonexistent shortage of trained and qualified Americans.

University of California computer science professor Norm Matloff, who watches this issue closely, said that Cohen & Grigsby's practices are the standard ones used by hordes of attorneys, who are making money by putting Americans out of work.

The Cohen & Grigsby video was a short-term sensation as it undermined the business propaganda that no American employee was being displaced by foreigners on H-1b or L-1 work visas. Soon, however, business organizations and their shills were back in gear lying to Congress and the public about the amazing shortage of qualified Americans for literally every technical and professional occupation, especially IT and software engineering.

Everywhere we hear the same droning lie from business interests that there are not enough American engineers and scientists. For mysterious reasons educated Americans prefer to be waitresses and bartenders, hospital orderlies, and retail clerks.

As one of the few who writes about this short-sighted policy of American managers endeavoring to maximize their "performance bonuses," I receive much feedback from affected Americans. Many responses come from recent university graduates such as the one who "graduated nearly at the top of my class in 2002" with degrees in both electrical and computer engineering and who "hasn't been able to find a job."

The hundreds of individual cases that have been brought to my attention are dismissed as "anecdotal" by my fellow economists. So little do they know. I also receive numerous responses from American engineers and IT workers who have managed to hold on to jobs or to find new ones after long intervals when they have been displaced by foreign hires. Their descriptions of their work environments are fascinating.

For example, Dayton, Ohio, was once home to numerous American engineers. Today, writes one surviving American, "I feel like an alien in my own country—as if Dayton had been colonized by India. NCR and other local employers have either offshored most of their IT work or rely heavily on Indian guest workers. The IT department of National City Bank across the street from LexisNexis is entirely Indian. The nearby apartment complexes house large numbers of Indian guest workers filling the engineering needs of many area businesses."

On November 6, 2006, Michael S. Teitelbaum, vice president of the Alfred P. Sloan Foundation, explained to a subcommittee of the House Committee on Science and Technology the difference between the conventional or false portrait that there is a shortage of US scientists and engineers and reality. The reality, Teitelbaum explained, is that the combination of offshoring, foreign guest workers, and educational subsidies have produced a surplus of US engineers and scientists that leaves many facing unstable and failed careers.

As two examples of the false portrait, Teitelbaum cited the 2005 report, *Tapping America's Potential*, led by the Business Roundtable and signed onto by 14 other business associations, and the 2006 National Academies report, *Rising Above the Gathering Storm*, "which was the basis for substantial parts of what eventually evolved into the American COMPETES Act."

Teitelbaum posed the question to the US Representatives: "Why do you continue to hear energetic re-assertions of the Conventional Portrait of 'shortages,' shortfalls, failures of K-12 science and math teaching, declining interest among US students [in science and engineering], and the necessity of importing more foreign scientists and engineers?"

Teitelbaum's answer: "In my judgment, what you are hearing is simply the expressions of interests by interest groups and their lobbyists. This phenomenon is, of course, very familiar to everyone on the Hill. Interest groups that are well organized and funded have the capacity to make their claims heard by you, either directly or via echoes in the mass press. Meanwhile those who are not well-organized and funded can express their views, but only as individuals."

Using the biomedical research sector as an example, Teitelbaum explained to the congressmen how research funding creates an oversupply of scientists that requires ever larger funding to keep employed. Teitelbaum made it clear that it is nonsensical to simultaneously increase the supply of American scientists while forestalling their employment with a shortage myth that is used to import foreigners on work visas.

Integrity is so lacking in America that the shortage myth serves the short-term financial interests of universities, funding agencies, employers, and immigration attorneys at the expense of American students, whose economic prospects are harmed by their naive pursuit of professions in which their prospects are dim. Initially it was blue-collar factory workers who were abandoned by US corporations and politicians. Now it is white-collar employees and Americans trained in science and technology.

Congress has had a parade of CEOs, ranging from Bill Gates of Microsoft and IBM executives on down the line, to testify that they desperately need more H-1B work visas for foreign employees as they cannot find enough American software engineers and IT workers to grow their businesses. Yet, all the companies who sing this song have established records of replacing American employees with H-1B workers.

For example, in 2009 Microsoft, IBM, Texas Instruments, Sprint Nextel, Intel, Motorola, and scores of other corporations announced thousands of layoffs of the qualified American engineers who "are in short supply."

IBM has offered to help to relocate its "redundant" but "scarce" American engineers to its operations in India, China, Brazil, Mexico, the Czech Republic, Russia, South Africa, Nigeria, and the United Arab Emirates at the salaries prevailing in those countries.[41]

On January 28, 2009, *USA Today* reported: "In 2007, the last full year for which detailed employment numbers are available, 121,000 of IBM's 387,000 workers [31%] were in the U.S. Meanwhile, staffing in India has jumped from just 9,000 workers in 2003 to 74,000 workers in 2007."

In order to penetrate and to serve foreign markets, US corporations need overseas operations. There is nothing unusual or unpatriotic about direct foreign investment in plant and equipment. However, many US companies use foreign labor to manufacture abroad the products that they sell in American markets. If Henry Ford had used Indian, Chinese, or Mexican workers to manufacture his cars, Indians, Chinese and Mexicans could possibly have purchased Fords, but not Americans.

In 2009 US Senators Charles Grassley and Bernie Sanders offered an amendment to the Troubled Asset Relief Program (TARP) bill that would prevent companies receiving bailout money from discharging American employees and replacing them with foreigners on H-1B visas.

The U.S. Chamber of Commerce and immigration advocates, such as the American Immigration Lawyers Association, immediately went to work to defeat or to water down the amendment. Senator Grassley's attempt to prevent American corporations from replacing American workers with foreigners on H-1B work visas in the midst of the most serious economic crisis since the Great Depression was met with outrage from the U.S. Chamber of Commerce, an organization determined to protect the multi-million dollar bonuses paid to American CEOs for reducing labor costs by replacing their American employees with foreign employees.

On January 23, 2009, Senator Grassley wrote to Microsoft CEO Steve Ballmer:

> I am concerned that Microsoft will be retaining foreign guest workers rather than similarly qualified American employees when it implements its layoff plan. As you know, I

want to make sure employers recruit qualified American workers first before hiring foreign guest workers. For example, I cosponsored legislation to overhaul the H-1B and L-1 visa programs to give priority to American workers and to crack down on unscrupulous employers who deprive qualified Americans of high-skilled jobs. Fraud and abuse is rampant in these programs, and we need more transparency to protect the integrity of our immigration system.

Last year, Microsoft was here on Capitol Hill advocating for more H-1B visas. The purpose of the H-1B visa program is to assist companies in their employment needs where there is not a sufficient American workforce to meet their technology expertise requirements. However, H-1B and other work visa programs were never intended to replace qualified American workers. Certainly, these work visa programs were never intended to allow a company to retain foreign guest workers rather than similarly qualified American workers, when that company cuts jobs during an economic downturn.

It is imperative that in implementing its layoff plan, Microsoft ensures that American workers have priority in keeping their jobs over foreign workers on visa programs.

My point is that during a layoff, companies should not be retaining H-1B or other work visa program employees over qualified American workers. Our immigration policy is not intended to harm the American workforce. I encourage Microsoft to ensure that Americans are given priority in job retention. Microsoft has a moral obligation to protect these American workers by putting them first during these difficult economic times.

Senator Grassley is rightly concerned that recession layoffs will shield increased jobs offshoring and use of H-1B workers. On February 13, 2009, Pravda reported that "America has begun the initial steps to final outsourcing of its last dominant industry"—oil/gas and oil/gas services. Pravda reports that "as with other formerly dominant industries, such as light manufacturing, IT, textiles," recession is "used as the knife to finally do in the workers."

According to Pravda,

IT (Information Technology) is a prime example. The companies used the dot.com bust to lay off hundreds of thousands of tech workers around the US and Britain, citing low profits or debt. The public as a whole accepted this, as part of the economic landscape and protests were few, especially with a prospect of the situation turning around. However, shortly after the turn around in the economy, it became very clear that there would be no turn around in the IT employment industry. Not only were companies outsourcing everything they could, under the cover of the recession, they had shipped in tens of thousands of H-1B work visaed workers who were paid on the cheap.[42]

It is rare to find US Representatives and Senators,

such as Grassley, who will take a stand against powerful special interests. Some do so inadvertently, forgetting that patriotism is no longer a characteristic of the American business elite. Hoping to stimulate American rather than foreign businesses, the House version of the economic stimulus bill, the American Recovery and Reinvestment Act of 2009, required that funds provided by the bill cannot be used to purchase foreign-made iron, steel, and textiles.

The Senate provision was more sweeping, mandating that all manufactured goods purchased with stimulus money be American-made.

The U.S. Chamber of Commerce, the National Association of Manufacturers, Caterpillar, General Electric, other transnational corporations, and editorial writers, whose newspapers are owned by corporate interests or are dependent on corporate advertising, set out to defeat the buy American requirement. As far as these anti-American organizations are concerned, the stimulus bill has nothing to do with American jobs or the American economy. It only has to do with the special interest appetites that have the political power to rip off the American taxpayers.[43]

Representing the corporate interests, Senator John McCain declared the Senate provision to be "protectionism" and harmful to America. McCain alleged that the buy American provision would cause a second Great Depression. U.S. Chamber of Commerce President Thomas Donohue said that buying foreign-made goods was "economic patriotism." President Obama even appointed apologists for jobs offshoring to his National Economic Council. The American economic elite hide their treason to the American people behind "free trade."

The ruins of America's once great manufacturing and industrial cities stand as monuments to the success that the US Chamber of Commerce and global corporations have had "in saving Americans from protectionism." According to the 2010 US census data, the population of Detroit, Michigan, once America's 4th largest city and a powerhouse of US manufacturing, declined by 25% in the first decade of the 21st century. With large areas of the once great city consisting of abandoned buildings and houses, the city is attempting to shrink its borders by 40 square miles.

In the first decade of the 21st century, Gary, Indiana, lost 22% of its population. Flint, Michigan, lost 18%. Cleveland, Ohio, lost 17%. Pittsburgh, Pennsylvania lost 7%, South Bend, Indiana, lost 6%, and Rochester, New York, lost 4%. These cities were once the home of American manufacturing and industrial might.

Between 1990 and 2010, St. Louis, Missouri, lost 20% of its population, and 19% of its housing units stand vacant. As the United States' ability to make things disappears, the hubris of America's leaders rises as they fancy themselves to be a hegemonic superpower. Photographs of the ruins that now comprise what once were centers of US productive might are abundantly supplied on the Internet. See, for example, "The Ruins of Detroit."[44]

Where Did the Money Go?

The wealth that has been extracted by jobs offshoring and financial fraud has reappeared in "Richistan," a new country within America. Author Robert Frank describes the new world of the super-rich and their fantastic conspicuous consumption.

In Richistan there is a two-year waiting list for $50 million 200-foot yachts. In Richistan expensive Rolex watches are considered Wal-Mart junk. Richistanians sport $736,000 Franck Muller timepieces on their wrists, sign their names with $700,000 Mont Blanc jewel-encrusted pens. Their valets, butlers (with $100,000 salaries), and bodyguards carry the $42,000 Louis Vitton handbags of wives and mistresses.

Richistanians join clubs open only to those with $100 million, pay $650,000 for golf club memberships, eat $50 hamburgers and $1,000 omelettes, drink $90 a bottle Bling mineral water and down $10,000 "martinis on a rock" (gin or vodka poured over a diamond) at New York's Algonquin Hotel.

Who are the Richistanians? They are CEOs who have moved their companies abroad and converted the wages they formerly paid Americans into $100 million compensation packages for themselves. They are investment bankers and hedge fund managers, who created and marketed the subprime mortgage derivatives that brought financial crisis to the world. One of them was paid $1.7 *billion* in 2006. The $575 million that each of 25 other top earners were paid is paltry by comparison, but unimaginable wealth to everyone else.

The real wages and salaries of Americans who are not Richistanians are lower than a decade or several decades ago. With their debts at all time highs, with the prices of their main asset—their homes—collapsing from overbuilding, fraudulent finance, and foreclosures, and with scant opportunities to rise for the children they struggled to educate, Americans who are not privileged Richistanians face a dim future.

The financial crisis was piled on top of the devastation inflicted on Americans by jobs offshoring. The debt monetization that accompanies this crisis threatens Americans with inflation and the US dollar with the loss of its role as world reserve currency. The large federal budget deficits threaten the social safety net and the pension (Social Security) and health care (Medicare) systems for the elderly. Once again, the gains for a few come at the expense of the loss of the many.

Fraud by Banksters

Matt Taibbi (*Griftopia*, 2010) and Gretchen Morgenson and Joshua Rosner (*RECKLESS Endangerment*, 2011) document the financial crisis associated with subprime derivatives and credit default swaps as the result of stupidity, greed, and criminality on the part of both government policymakers and financial executives.

The US government set the crisis in motion with the repeal in 1999 of the Glass-Steagall Act, which had kept commercial and investment banking separated since 1933.

Deregulation of the derivatives market followed. Soon fraud was running rampant, and debt was leveraged to irresponsible heights. The incompetent fools responsible for these "financial reforms" were portrayed in the media as heroes of Caesarian stature.

Mortgage securitization was the vehicle that spread Wall Street's fraudulent "securities" around the world. Securitization allows lenders to issue mortgages for fees and to sell the mortgages to third parties, who combine them with mortgages from other lenders. The collection of mortgages is then sold to investors. Securitization removed the risk of payment failure from lenders, who thus became less concerned with the credit-worthiness of borrowers.

In order to reassure investors about credit-worthiness and to appeal to risk-tolerant hedge funds, the next development was to take a pool of mortgages of varying credit-worthiness and to organize them into three tranches. The mortgages were separated into AAA, B grade, and high-risk. The triple A tranche could be sold to pension funds and institutional investors. Hedge funds would take the high-risk tranche for the high-interest rate that they offered, intending to get rid of the mortgages before they had time to go bad. The middle tranche was the one hard to sell. The interest rate on the B grade tranche was not high enough to appeal to hedge funds, and pension funds were restricted to investment grade.

So what did the banksters do? They lumped together all the B grade tranches and repeated the process all over. The best of the lot were turned into—you guessed it—AAA, then came the B grade, and then the worst of the lot became the third tranche. And then the process was repeated again.

This was bad enough, but even worse was happening. Many of the AAA and B grade mortgages had that rating only because of fraudulent credit scores that lenders created for borrowers and because Wall Street rating agencies assigned investment grade ratings to lower grade mortgages. The rating agencies are not independent of Wall Street. The rating agencies are paid a fee by the issuers of financial paper for the ratings. Everyone was focused on short-term profits, from the lenders who churned out mortgages for fees, to rating agencies that churned out ratings for fees, to hedge funds that had no intention of holding the high-risk tranches beyond the short-run. This is how "toxic waste" was spread throughout the financial system.

Then it became possible to "insure" the AAA mortgages (many of which were not AAA). Once this happened, financial institutions that were required to maintain reserves against deposits or to capitalize obligations, such as insurance policies, could now substitute higher-paying mortgage derivatives for U.S. Treasury notes and still meet their reserve requirements for a ready cash reserve. Treasury notes are so liquid that they are considered the equivalent of cash, and insured AAA securitized mortgages acquired similar status.

The insurance company, AIG, became the big provider of "insurance" in an operation run by Joe Cassano. Taibbi's account is masterful. Cassano's "insurance" product is called a credit default swap (CDS). It was not insurance, because AIG did not set aside capital to pay any claims. And claims there would be. Not only were the AAA mortgages that were being insured littered with subprime derivatives and other toxic waste, but also investment banks and hedge funds could purchase swaps against debt instruments that they did not even own. As Taibbi puts it, people were gambling in a casino in which gamblers did not have to cover their bets or own the financial instruments that they were insuring by purchasing credit default swaps.

While Cassano was collecting fees for bets that he could not cover, Win Neuger on the other side of AIG was lending the insurance giant's long-term portfolio of sound investments to short-sellers for a fee.

Short-selling works like this: A short-seller has a hunch or inside information that a company's stock price is going to fall in value. He borrows the stock from AIG or some other company by putting up collateral equal to its market price on the day the stock is borrowed plus a small fee. Then he sells the stock, pockets the money and waits for the stock to fall. If his hunch or inside information is correct, and the stock falls in value, he buys the stock and returns it to AIG, pocketing the difference in the two prices.

Normally, people who lend stock to short-sellers are content with the fee and with the interest on the collateral (cash) invested in safe instruments like Treasury bills. The lender of the stock cannot take any risk with the cash collateral, because the cash must be returned to the short-seller when he returns the borrowed stock.

However, once questionable financial instruments got AAA ratings from Wall Street rating agencies plus insurance from AIG, these dubious financial instruments could displace US Treasuries as a place for Neuger to hold the short-sellers' collateral. You can see the untenable position into which Cassano and Neuger put AIG.

Enter Goldman Sachs as a buyer of swaps from Cassano and a borrower of stocks from Neuger. Once the real estate bubble popped that the crazed Federal Reserve had caused, all the fraud that had been hidden by rising real estate prices appeared in its naked glory. AIG could not cover Cassano's swaps, and it could not return to short-sellers their collateral that Neuger had invested in subprime derivatives.

This was the origin of the 2008 Troubled Asset Relief Program (TARP) bailout. Goldman Sachs (whose former executives, as Taibbi relates, controlled the U.S. Treasury, financial regulatory agencies, and the Federal Reserve) perceived a bailout as an opportunity to have U.S. taxpayers pay off AIG's losing bets with Goldman Sachs and also fund with free capital supplied by the bailout more money-making opportunities for "banks too big to fail."

As Taibbi shows, Goldman Sachs had yet more ruin to bring to America and the world. Goldman Sachs managed to get the position limits repealed that regulation imposed on speculators. Position limits served to prevent speculation from taking over commodity markets (for example, grains, metals, and oil). Position limits on speculators limited the number of options or future contracts speculators could accumulate. The repeal of the limits allowed Goldman Sachs to create a new product, index speculation, which brought hundreds of billions of dollars of speculative money into commodities markets, allowing speculators to dominate commodity markets and to manipulate commodity markets as they do equity, debt, and currency markets.

There is much evidence of fraud and criminality on the part of financial firms and of conflicts of interest on the part of government policymakers, but no one has been held accountable and no meaningful corrective regulation has been enacted. The financial system remains a casino.

The Conflict of Interest that Masquerades as Government

One hallmark of a failed state is that the crooks are inside the government, using government to protect and to advance their private interests. Another hallmark is rising income inequality as the insiders manipulate economic policy for their enrichment at the expense of everyone else.

As noted above, income inequality in the US is now extreme. The 2008 Organization for Economic Co-operation and Development (OECD) report, "Income Distribution and Poverty in OECD Countries,"[43] concludes that the US is the country with the highest inequality and poverty rate across the OECD and that since 2000 nowhere has there been such a stark rise in income inequality as in the US. The OECD finds that in the US the distribution of wealth is even more unequal than the distribution of income.

On October 21, 2009, *Business Week* highlighted a new report from the United Nations Development Program that concluded that the US ranked third among states with the worst income inequality. As number one and number two, Hong Kong and Singapore, are both essentially city states, not countries, the US actually has the shame of being the country with the most inequality in the distribution of income.

The stark increase in US income inequality in the 21st century coincides with the offshoring of US jobs, which enriched executives with "performance bonuses" while impoverishing the middle class, and with the rapid rise of unregulated over-the-counter (OTC) derivatives and extraordinary debt leverage, which enriched Wall Street and the financial sector at the expense of everyone else.

Many critics of the worsening income and wealth distribution place the blame on President George W. Bush's tax cuts, which were extended by Congress and President Obama. As the richest 1% receive much of their income in the form of capital gains, the reduction in the capital gains tax rate to 15% helped to worsen the inequality. However, the emphasis on taxation ignores the impact that two decades of jobs offshoring has had on the distribution of income and wealth. Taxing the rich cannot redress the loss of income for most Americans caused by moving US jobs offshore and by the conversion of that income into executive pay and shareholder's capital gains.

The OECD report shows that the rate of increase in US income inequality declined during the Reagan years despite the tax rate reductions. During the mid-1990s the Gini coefficient (the measure of income inequality) actually fell. Beginning in 2000 with the New Economy (essentially financial fraud and offshoring of US jobs), the Gini coefficient shot up sharply.

While income and wealth accumulates at the top, millions of Americans have lost their homes and half of their retirement savings, while being loaded up with government debt to bail out the banksters who created the crisis.

Frontline's TV broadcast, "The Warning," documents how Federal Reserve Chairman Alan Greenspan, Treasury Secretary Robert Rubin, Deputy Treasury Secretary Larry Summers, and Securities and Exchange Commission Chairman Arthur Levitt blocked Brooksley Born, head of the Commodity Futures Trading Commission (CFTC), from performing her statutory duties and regulating over-the-counter (OTC) derivatives.[46]

After the worst crisis in US financial history struck, just as Brooksley Born predicted, a disgraced Federal Reserve Chairman, Alan Greenspan, was summoned out of retirement to explain to Congress his unequivocal assurances that no regulation of derivatives was necessary. Greenspan had even told Congress that regulation of derivatives would be harmful. A pathetic Greenspan had to admit that the free market ideology on which he had relied turned out to have a flaw.

Greenspan may have bet America's economy on his free market ideology, but does anyone believe that Rubin and Summers were doing anything other than protecting the enormous fraud-based profits that derivatives were bringing Wall Street? As Brooksley Born stressed, OTC derivatives are a "dark market." There is no transparency. Regulators have no information on them and neither do purchasers.

Even after Long Term Capital Management failed in 1998 and had to be bailed out, Greenspan, Rubin, and Summers stuck to their guns. Greenspan, Rubin and Summers, and a gullible Securities and Exchange Commission Chairman, Arthur Levitt, who now regrets that he was the banksters' dupe, succeeded in manipulating Congress into blocking the CFTC from doing its mandated job. Brooksley Born, prevented by the public's elected representatives from protecting the public, resigned. Wall Street money simply shoved facts and honest regulators aside, resulting in the financial crisis that hit in 2008 and continues to plague the economy today.

The financial insiders running the Treasury, White House, and Federal Reserve shifted to taxpayers the cost of the catastrophe that they had created. When the crisis hit, Henry Paulson, appointed by President George W. Bush to be Rubin's replacement as the Goldman Sachs representative running the US Treasury, hyped fear to obtain from "the people's representatives" in Congress, with no questions asked, hundreds of billions of taxpayers' dollars (TARP money) to bail out Goldman Sachs and the other malefactors of unregulated derivatives.

When Goldman Sachs announced that it was paying massive six and seven figure bonuses to every employee, public outrage erupted. In defense of banksters, saved with the public's money, paying themselves bonuses in excess of most people's life-time earnings, Lord Griffiths, the British Vice Chairman of Goldman Sachs International, said that the public must learn to "tolerate the inequality as a way to achieve greater prosperity for all."

In other words, "Let them eat cake."

According to the UN report cited above, Great Britain has the 7th most unequal income distribution in the world. After the Goldman Sachs bonuses, the British will move up in distinction, perhaps rivaling Israel for the fourth spot in the hierarchy.

Despite the absurdity of unregulated derivatives, the high level of public anger, and Greenspan's confession to Congress that his theory has a flaw, still nothing has been done to regulate derivatives. One of Rubin's Assistant Treasury Secretaries, Gary Gensler, replaced Brooksley Born as head of the CFTC. Larry Summers was appointed head of President Obama's National Economic Council. Former Federal Reserve official Timothy Geithner, a Paulson protege, was appointed Treasury Secretary. A Goldman Sachs vice president, Adam Storch, was appointed the chief operating officer of the Securities and Exchange Commission. The Banksters remain in charge.

Is there another country in which, in full public view, a handful of insiders so blatantly use government for the enrichment of private interests, with a coterie of "free market" economists available to justify plunder on the grounds that "the market knows best"? A narco-state is bad enough. The US surpasses this horror with its financo-state.

As Brooksley Born says, if nothing is done "it'll happen again."

But nothing can be done. The crooks have the government.

Death by Globalism

Economists have made themselves irrelevant. If you have any doubts, have a look at the 2010 summer issue of the magazine, *International Economy*, a publication endorsed by former Federal Reserve chairmen Paul Volcker and Alan Greenspan, by Jean-Claude Trichet, former president of the European Central Bank, by former Secretary of State George Shultz, and by *The New York Times* and *Washington Post*.

The main feature is "The Great Stimulus Debate," which addresses the question: Is the Obama fiscal stimulus helping the economy or hindering it? Princeton economics professor and New York Times columnist Paul Krugman and Moody's Analytics chief economist Mark Zandi represent the Keynesian view that government deficit spending is needed to lift the economy out of recession. Zandi declares that thanks to the fiscal stimulus, "The economy has made enormous progress since early 2009," a mistaken opinion shared by the President Obama's Council of Economic Advisors and the Congressional Budget Office.

The opposite view, associated with Harvard economics professor Robert Barro and with European economists, such as Francesco Giavazzi and Marco Pagano and the European Central Bank, is that government budget surpluses achieved by cutting government spending spur the economy by reducing the ratio of debt to Gross Domestic Product. This is the "let them eat cake school of economics."

Barro says that fiscal stimulus has no effect, because people anticipate the future tax increases implied by government deficits and increase their personal savings to offset the added government debt. Giavazzi and Pagano reason that since fiscal stimulus does not expand the economy, fiscal austerity consisting of higher taxes and reduced government spending could be the cure for unemployment.

If one overlooks the real world and the need of life for sustenance, one can become engrossed in this debate. However, the minute one looks out the window upon the world, one realizes that cutting Social Security, Medicare, Medicaid, food stamps, and housing subsidies is a certain path to death by starvation, curable diseases, and exposure when 15 million or more Americans have lost jobs, medical coverage, and homes. Although some proponents of this anti-Keynesian policy deny that it results in social upheaval, Gerald Celente's observation is closer to the mark: "When people have nothing left to lose, they lose it."

The Krugman Keynesian school is just as deluded. Neither side in "The Great Stimulus Debate" has a clue that the problem for the U.S. is that a large chunk of U.S. GDP and the jobs, incomes, and careers associated with it, have been moved offshore and given to Chinese, Indians, and others with low wage rates. Corporate profits have soared, while job prospects for the middle class have been eliminated.

The offshoring of American jobs resulted from (1) Wall Street pressures on corporations for "higher shareholder earnings," that is, for more profits, and from (2) no-think economists, such as the ones engaged in the debate over fiscal stimulus, who mistakenly associate globalism with free trade instead of with its antithesis—the pursuit of lowest factor cost abroad or absolute advantage.

As economists assume, incorrectly, that free trade is always mutually beneficial, economists have failed to examine the devastatingly harmful effects of offshoring. The more intelligent among them who point it out are dismissed as "protectionists."

The reason fiscal stimulus cannot rescue the U.S. economy has nothing to do with the difference between Barro and Krugman. It has to do with the fact that a large percentage of high-productivity, high-value-added jobs and the middle class incomes and careers associated with them have been given to foreigners. What used to be U.S. GDP is now Chinese, Indian, and other country GDP. When the jobs have been shipped overseas, fiscal stimulus cannot put unemployed workers back to work.

The "let them eat cake school" is equally off the mark. As jobs, investment, research and development have been moved offshore, cutting the social safety net simply drives the domestic population deeper in the ground. Americans cannot pay their mortgages, car payments, tuition, utility bills, or for that matter, any bill, based on Chinese and Indian pay scales. Therefore, Americans are priced out of the labor market and become dependencies of the federal budget. "Fiscal consolidation" means writing off large numbers of humans.

During the Great Depression, many wage and salary earners were new members of the labor force arriving from family farms, where many parents and grandparents still supported themselves. When their city jobs disappeared, many could return to the farm.

Today farming is in the hands of agri-business corporations. There are no farms to which the unemployed can return.

The "let them eat cake school" never mentions the one point in its favor. The US, with all its huffed up power and importance, depends on the US dollar as reserve currency. It is this role of the dollar that allows America to pay for its imports in its own currency. For a country whose trade is as unbalanced as America's, the reserve currency privilege keeps the country afloat.

The threats to the dollar's role are the budget and trade deficits. Both are so large and have accumulated for so long that the ability to make good on them is in doubt. As I have written for a number of years, the US is so heavily dependent on the dollar as reserve currency that the US must have as its main policy goal to preserve the dollar in that role. Otherwise, the US, an import-dependent country, will be unable to pay for its excess of imports over its exports.

"Fiscal consolidation," the new term for austerity, could save the dollar. However, unless starvation, homelessness and social upheaval are acceptable consequences, the austerity must fall on the military budget. America cannot afford its multi-trillion dollar wars that serve only to enrich those invested in the armaments industries. The U.S. cannot afford the neoconservative dream of world hegemony and a conquered Middle East open to Israeli colonization.

Is anyone surprised that not a single proponent of the "let them eat cake school" mentions cutting military spending? Entitlements (Social Security and Medicare), despite the fact that they are paid for by earmarked payroll taxes and have been in surplus since the Reagan administration, are always what economists put on the chopping bloc.

Where do the two schools stand on inflation vs. deflation? We don't have to worry. Martin Feldstein, one of America's pre-eminent economists, says: "The good news is that investors should worry about neither." His explanation epitomizes the insouciance of American economists.

Feldstein says that there cannot be inflation because of the high rate of unemployment and the low rate of capacity utilization. Thus, "there is little upward pressure on wages and prices in the United States."

As for deflation, no risk there either. The huge deficits prevent deflation, "so the good news is that the possibility of significant inflation or deflation during the next few years is low on the list of economic risks faced by the U.S. economy and by financial investors."

What we have in front of us is an unaware economics profession. There might be some initial period of deflation as a result of weak consumer demand. The deflation would be short lived, because the prospect of financing a $1.5 trillion annual deficit evaporates once individual investors complete their flight from the stock market into "safe" government bonds, once the hyped Greek, Spanish, and Italian sovereign debt crises have driven investors out of euros into dollars, and once the banks' excess reserves created by the bailout have been used up in the purchase of Treasuries.

Then what finances the deficit? Who purchases the next $1.5 trillion tranche of US Treasuries in order to cover the budgetary red ink? Don't look for an answer from either side of The Great Stimulus Debate. Economists haven't a clue despite the fact that the answer is obvious.

The Federal Reserve will monetize the federal government deficit, as it has been doing. The result of printing money in the absence of employment opportunities, should the money get past the banks and into the economy, would be to combine high inflation with high unemployment. Another path to high inflation would be through a decline in the dollar's exchange value, which would raise the prices of imports. The rest of the world observing the unending creation of new debt and money in Washington could decide to unload their dollar holdings, thereby causing a decline in the dollar's exchange value.

The no-think economists, who have been cheerleaders for deregulation and globalism, have no comprehension that they have created a perfect storm. If the Federal Reserve ceases to print money with which to purchase bonds, interest rates would rise, and the bond and stock markets would collapse. Unemployment would rise. The budget deficit would widen. There could be a run on the dollar. If the Federal Reserve continues to print money, the supply of dollars will continue to grow faster than the demand for dollars, with obvious implications for the exchange value of the dollar.

PART III

THE END
OF SOVEREIGNTY

The European sovereign debt crisis is being used to achieve three goals: to protect bankers from their mistakes by passing the cost to the European peoples; to change the rules under which the European Central Bank operates; and to terminate the economic and political sovereignty of the European Union member countries.

The European financial crisis originated with Wall Street's marketing of junk financial instruments with fraudulent investment grade ratings. Goldman Sachs used Enron-style accounting to hide the extent of Greece's public debt so that the Greek government could continue to borrow within the EU rules. When it was discovered that German, French, and Dutch banks held not only Wall Street's junk "securities," but also Greek, Spanish, Italian, Irish, and Portuguese (PIIGS) sovereign debt in excess of what the countries could service, the second stage of the debt crisis hit.

The US and the UK are countries with their own currencies, and their central banks can create money in order to extend credit to the governments. In contrast, members of the European Union share a common currency. The central banks of the member countries cannot create euros in order to serve as creditors to the governments. European Union member governments are dependent on private banks to finance their deficits.

The EU has rules governing the permissible size of member countries' budget deficits. However, a number of member countries have succeeded in evading the limits. The European Central Bank (ECB) is prohibited by its charter from financing the deficits of member countries. Regardless of the rules, the sovereign debt crisis has caused the ECB to assent to bailout schemes that violate its charter by requiring the ECB to lend in support of Greek sovereign debt.

The initial response to the Greek sovereign debt crisis was to prevent the private German, French, and Dutch banks from losing any money. Instead of restructuring and writing down part of Greece's public debt, the decision was made to impose severe austerity on the Greek population. Wages, pensions, and employment were reduced, and Greece was told to sell its state lottery, municipal water companies, and the country's ports. Islands that are part of the national heritage would be sold to real estate developers. The funds expected from the austerity and privatization package would be used to repay the ECB and IMF for loans that enable the Greek government to repay the private banks.

The Greek population revolted, taking to the streets and resisting the police with Molotov cocktails. When the private banks agreed to write down part of the Greek debt in exchange for capital infusions from EU taxpayers and Greece's submission to an International Monetary Fund austerity package, Greek Prime Minister George Papandreou said he would respond to the people's protests by letting them vote on the deal.

This caused an uproar from Europe's political elite and EU pressure on Prime Minister Papandreou to resign. Italy's Prime Minister Berlusconi suffered a similar fate. According to news reports, Germany's Merkel and France's

Sarkozy congratulated themselves on removing from office the prime ministers of Greece and Italy.

This is not democracy; it is the contempt of democracy. However, the greatest threat to self-rule in Europe comes from the ECB's response to the Greek debt crisis.

In 13th century England when peasants were uprooted from the land that had provided their sustenance for centuries, we don't know what rhetoric elites used to disguise expropriation by "fire and sword." Eight centuries later with expropriation again underway, the rhetoric is Orwellian. Today the peasants in Greece, Ireland, and Spain are being expropriated by having their wages and pensions cut, their taxes raised, their jobs abolished, their social services slashed, and their social infrastructure privatized in the name of "making democracy work," "rescuing Greek finances," "winning a bailout," "saving the Euro," "internal devaluation," "free market reform," and "avoiding contagion."

Economist Michael Hudson calls it "financialized neofeudalism." Peoples are being enserfed and economies destroyed all in order that bankers don't have to suffer losses on their casino gambling bets.

Not only is the process immoral, but also it is illegal. The European Central Bank (ECB) and the International Monetary Fund (IMF) are illegally supplying the funds to bailout the German, French, and Dutch banks that hold the Greek government's bonds. The treaties that created the European Union prohibit the ECB from bailing out EU member governments. The IMF Articles of Agreement prevent the IMF from lending to governments for the purpose of fiscal or budgetary support. IMF loans are restricted to balance of payments loans when a country lacks the foreign exchange reserves to cover a deficit in its balance of payments. Greece's problem is not its balance of payments.

Despite the legal clarity, the charters of both financial organizations are being ignored for no other reason than to prevent bankers from having to pay for their own mistakes.

Lacking their own central banks that can extend credit to the government by monetizing the government's debt, the PIIGS do not have "quantitative easing"—the purchase of the government's debt by its own central bank—as an option open to them.

Bankers bought more Greek debt than Greece can pay interest on, roll over, or retire. Normally what would happen in such a case is that the debt is restructured and reduced to an amount that the debtor is able to pay. This involves the holders of the bonds taking a haircut by having to write down losses on their investments. However, the bankers now have sufficient power to transfer the cost of their own mistakes to the general public.

In Greece's case, the banker-preferred solution is that the ECB and IMF violate the rules under which they are supposed to operate and lend enough money to Greece in order that Greece can repay the bankers with more borrowed money. Indeed, it is even worse than that.

Obviously, if Greece cannot make its bonds good, Greece cannot repay the loans from the ECB and IMF. For the scheme to go forward, the Greek government has to be coerced into permitting private interests, that is, the bankers or the bankers' customers, to plunder Greece by acquiring the state lottery, the country's ports, postal service, the water companies of municipalities, and a collection of Greek islands. The banks, or business interests funded with bank loans, expect to purchase the public sector of Greece on favorable terms.

In addition, the Greek government has been told to free up tax revenues with which to repay the ECB and IMF loans by laying off public employees, cutting their pensions, raising taxes, and slashing the remaining public services. The money and income flows leave Greece and go to foreign bankers, driving the Greek economy deeper into recession and inability to pay.

Needless to say, the Greek population opposed the austerity that is mandated in order to receive what *The New York Times* called in the summer of 2011 the prize of "winning a bailout." The winner, of course, is not Greece, but the German, Dutch, and French bankers. This is why Greeks, who have been protesting in the streets, were further enraged to discover that their socialist government represents foreign banks and not Greek citizens.

The Greek government aligned with the foreign bankers. On June 23, 2011, the Greek finance minister "won" the bailout, or perhaps more precisely a stage of the bailout, with a five-year austerity plan that lowers the minimum threshold for income tax to 8,000 euros a year, increases the tax on heating oil, and imposes a "solidarity levy" on income of between 1 and 5 percent. Obviously, the poor are being made to pay for the rich bankers' mistakes.

The "won" bailout was disrupted by Prime Minister Papandreou's endorsement of a referendum. With Papandreou forced out of office by the EU elite, Greece found itself with an appointed prime minister who was a former vice president of the European Central Bank. The European elite expect the new prime minister to sacrifice the Greek people to the bankers.

As I write the outcome of the European debt crisis is unknown. The effort to save the bankers, the EU and the euro with coerced austerity programs and illegal bailouts might succeed or fail. However, at time of writing, the most conclusive result of the crisis to date is that European elites have decided to terminate member countries sovereignty over budgets, taxing, and spending.

According to Jean-Claude Trichet, the leader of the ECB until November 2011, the next step in "making democracy work" is to remove the sovereignty of the Greek government. In a speech on June 2, 2011, Trichet said that the task was to bring Europe beyond a "strict concept of nationhood" and the traditional practice of protecting debtors. Whether a country could afford to pay its debts was no longer a question of its budgetary condition if the country has public domain that can be privatized.

Greece would have to be made to pay, said Trichet, or other EU member states would demand restructuring and write-downs of their excessive debts. In order to avoid a contagion of write-downs, which would be at the expense of creditor banks, the ECB was justified in disregarding its charter and providing the forbidden loans to Greece "in the context of a strong adjustment program." However, if the Greek government did not stick to the mandates of the adjustment program and sell off its public domain, a "second stage" of intervention would come into play. European Union authorities would exercise an "authoritative say in the formation of the country's economic policies."

EU interdependence, Trichet said, "means that countries *de facto* do not have complete internal authority." The "second stage" would make this *de jure*. European Union authorities would simply take over Greece's fiscal affairs and decide its budget. Sovereignty and representative government would be abrogated, and EU member states would come under the suzerainty of unaccountable rulers.

Much the same thing has happened in the US. Wall Street executives control the Treasury and financial regulatory agencies. Public money and the Federal Reserve's balance sheet were used to bail out the speculative and leveraged gambling bets of the irresponsible financial institutions. Government officials who arranged the bailout formerly headed the bailed out banks. Vast sums of money went to the banks, while millions of citizens lost their homes, jobs, pensions, and medical insurance. In the US direct democracy, in which the people decide by referendums, appears to be the only recourse to rule by the private interest groups that openly purchase the government in Washington.

The Greek "crisis" has not yet played out, despite the submission of the Greek government when its best option is simply to default and to leave the EU. Germans have been suspicious of monetary union from the start, because it removes control over inflation from their hands. As the bailouts of EU member countries by the ECB breach multiple clauses of EU treaty law, the bailouts breach the conditions on which Germany agreed to enter the European Union.

The pressure is on Merkel and Germany "to submit to realities" and to permit the monetization of debt that Germany has feared. The stakes for Germany are even higher. If the EU achieves the power to take over Greece's budget, as Trichet advocates, the EU obtains the power to put every member country's taxing and spending under its control. European countries will become like once independent American states, subservient to central power that rules from afar.

Does powerful Germany wish to cease to exist as an independent country? Are Germans content to assume the debt burdens of the PIIGS? If this is the price of Germany's membership in the European Union, what does Germany gain?

The Undeclared Agenda

The Greek drama that is playing out is both nonsensical and sinister. The bailout is not a bailout; it is a power play. The new loans are not designed to reduce

Greece's accumulated debt. The package merely creates new loans from the European Union and the International Monetary Fund to take the place of loans to Greece from private banks. The purpose of the bailout is not to rescue Greece, but to pay off the private banks that failed to do due diligence and lent more to a creditor than the creditor can repay. If Greece cannot repay the banks, it cannot repay the EU and IMF.

Greece, a country of 11 million people, had an estimated GDP of about $310 billion in 2010. According to the Hellenic Statistical Authority,[47] Greek GDP declined by almost 7% in 2011. With Greek GDP contracting more than forecast and the Greek budget deficit rising more than expected, the Greek government has been unable to meet the debt to GNP target ratios that are specified by the bailout plan.

Greek GDP decline is also forecast for 2012, the fourth consecutive year of economic contraction. On June 8, 2012, the Associated Press reported that Greek GDP contracted by 6.5% in the first quarter of 2012, an indication that the decline will be worse than forecast.

When GDP declines relative to the forecast used for the bailout and the budget deficit rises relative to the forecast, the ratio of debt to GDP rises despite the austerity measures. The attempt to reduce Greece's annual budget deficit and ratio of debt to GDP by imposing austerity measures, such as cutting pensions, wages, social services, and laying off government workers, causes aggregate demand and the economy to fall further, thus raising the ratio of debt to GDP.

Ever since John M. Keynes, economists have known that austerity measures are an unlikely solution to a weakening economy and rising budget deficits. So what is going on?

The "Greek debt crisis" is a "weapons of mass destruction" ruse to advance agendas that otherwise could not be pursued. We have seen what these agendas are: to solidify the principle already established in the US and Ireland that the general public, not shareholders, must bear the costs of bank losses; to give the ECB the power to monetize government debt; to use the crisis to destroy the sovereignty of the member countries of the EU.

The approach being taken to Greece's sovereign debt is one that the IMF imposes on third world countries with balance of payments problems due to persistent trade deficits. Greece is the first time this approach has been applied to sovereign debt. No explanation has been provided as to why the usual standard procedures for dealing with debt problems are not being used in Greece's case.

The reason I conclude that the "Greek debt crisis" is a ruse is that there are solutions that would solve the problem without the austerity and the looting which will *not* solve the problem. Normally, Greek debt would be restructured to fit the amount the country can repay. The rest would be written off.

If the amounts of the write-downs are large enough to wipe out the private banks' capital and leave the banks with insolvent balance sheets, there are easy solutions to this problem. One is to allow the banks to write down the bad debt over time as the profits of the banks allow. Instead of taking the hit all at once, the banks could spread it out over time, thus remaining solvent.

Another is for the European Central Bank to inject new capital into the banks instead of using its resources to lend money to Greece to hand over to the banks, money unlikely to be repaid.

Yet another is for the German, French, and Dutch governments to purchase their banks' bad debt, taking shares in the banks in return.

The value of any of these solutions is not only are they neater, easy to apply and less costly, but also they actually would solve the problem, because Greece's debt would be reduced.

Instead of reducing Greece's debt, the EU's scheme increases the debt relative to Greece's GDP as the economy declines under the austerity imposed. This suggests that the EU does not want to solve the Greek debt crisis, but to use the crisis to achieve more authority over member governments. The argument is that a common currency (the euro) requires the member states to have a common tax and budget policy set by Brussels.

Jean-Claude Trichet, the head of the European Central Bank, revealed the real agenda in his June 2, 2011 speech, when he said that the next step in the development of the European Union was to bring Europe beyond a "strict concept of nationhood."

This is the goal that the "Greek debt crisis" is being used to achieve. As Greece's economy continues to decline, Greece's ratio of debt to GDP will worsen. The EU will declare that it has no other recourse except to take over Greece's affairs. Greece will be the precedent that will then be applied to Italy, Spain, Portugal and, unless the EU is to become a Franco-Germanic Empire, eventually to France and Germany. The political sovereignty of the EU members will be erased. As the EU bureaucracy is essentially unaccountable, it means the end in all but name of representative government in Europe.

The US government is aiding and abetting this transition to tyranny. Washington fears that America's own troubled financial institutions have sold more credit default swaps against EU members' sovereign debt than the US banks can pay. A restructuring of Greek debt involving involuntary write downs would trigger the swap payments, whereas voluntary write downs by the banks as part of a deal does not trigger swap payments. However, a write down of

Greek debt could cause Spain, Italy, and Portugal to demand equal treatment. Thus the bank losses would grow.

Washington fears that swap payouts would worsen the US banking crisis and require more multi-trillion dollar loans from the Federal Reserve in order to prevent a collapse of banks "too big to fail." Therefore, Washington is in league with the EU in opposing debt restructuring. Washington has decided that tyranny in Europe is preferable to a deeper US financial crisis.

If the Greek protests evolve into open rebellion, the government could be overthrown. A successor government would have to repudiate the debt, thus halting for the time being the assault on the political sovereignty of the EU member states. The resistance of the Greek people caused EU authorities in the last months of 2011 to propose partial write-downs of Greek debt as part of the bailout deal.

The most likely outcome of the sovereign debt crisis will be an increase in EU authority over member countries. European Council President Herman Van Rompuy said that the sovereign debt crisis caused European authorities to reflect "on a further strengthening of economic convergence within the euro area, on improving fiscal discipline and deepening economic union, including exploring the possibility of limited Treaty changes." Van Rompuy's remarks indicate that member countries of the EU will become less independent in their decisions as they are merged into a single political entity.

In the meantime the bankers have taken over. The new president of the European Central Bank is Mario Draghi. This person was *Vice Chairman and Managing Director of Goldman Sachs International and a member of Goldman Sachs' Management Committee.* Draghi was also Italian Executive Director of the World Bank, Governor of the Bank of Italy, a member of the governing council of the European

Central Bank, a member of the board of directors of the Bank for International Settlements, and a member of the boards of governors of the International Bank for Reconstruction and Development and the Asian Development Bank, and Chairman of the Financial Stability Board.

Obviously, Draghi is going to protect the power of bankers.

Italy's new prime minister, who was appointed not elected, was *a member of Goldman Sachs Board of International Advisers.* Mario Monti was appointed to the European Commission, one of the governing organizations of the EU. Monti is European Chairman of the Trilateral Commission, a US organization that advances American hegemony over the world. Monti is a member of the Bilderberg group and a founding member of the Spinelli group, an organization created in September 2010 to facilitate integration within the EU. According to news reports, Monti's "technocratic cabinet" does not include a single elected politician. The banks are taking no chances: Monti is both prime minister and minister of economics and finance.

Just as an unelected banker was installed as prime minister of Italy, an unelected banker was installed as prime minister of Greece. Greece's new appointed prime minister, Lucas Papademos, was Governor of the Bank of Greece. From 2002-2010, he was Vice President of the European Central Bank. He also is a member of America's Trilateral Commission.

Jacques Delors, a founder of the European Union, promised the British Trade Union Congress in 1988 that the European Commission would require governments to introduce pro-labor legislation. Instead, we find the European Commission demanding that European labor bail out the private banks by accepting lower pay, fewer social services, and a later retirement.

Perhaps future historians will conclude that democracy once served the interests of money in order to break free of the power of kings, aristocracy, and government predations, but as money established control over governments, democracy became a liability. Historians will speak of the transition from the divine right of kings to the divine right of money.

Can Germany Remain a Sovereign Country?

Germany has been selected by the EU to provide the financial might to keep the EU glued together. A bailout fund is being established to which Germany is expected to contribute more than its share of the vote. Germans' inflation concerns are considered to be passé and a constraint on the development of the centralized European state in which European countries and history will simply disappear.

A great deal of money is behind this centralization of power, much of it American. A unified Europe is easier to control than a fractured one, and Europe, organized by the US into NATO, has become an auxiliary to America's Empire, fighting America's wars of hegemony in Central Asia and Africa.

What do Europeans have to gain? As Washington sends US Marines to Australia to counter China's rising power and surrounds nuclear-armed Russia with military and missile bases, Washington's imperial ambitions expose Europe's population and beautiful capital cities, depositories of centuries of art and architecture, to Russian nuclear weapons. What does Europe, beyond the payoff of its political "leaders," have to gain from Washington's hegemony?

Why is Europe lined up against Russia, the country that supplies Europeans with energy and markets for Europe's production? What does Washington do for Europe except to send its soldiers to die in foreign lands for American Empire?

The government of the US, and the military/security complex and neoconservatives that control it, see Europeans as dupes who can be pressured to sacrifice themselves for the handful of interest groups that control "the world's only superpower."

Europeans have their own identity. Why should they sacrifice it for a few American interest groups? If Europe is to be unified economically in a common market, the unity should extend to Russia. Germany should be finding its own destiny, not serving the special interests that control America.

The United States is a failed democracy. Washington has no concern for the economic welfare of citizens or for their civil liberties or for those of its European puppet states. Washington serves the purposes of the interest groups that control it. These interest groups are committed to financial fraud and to war.

CONCLUSION

This book demonstrates that empty-world economic theory has failed on its own terms and that its application by policymakers has resulted in the failure of capitalism itself. Pursuing absolute advantage in cheap labor abroad, First World corporations have wrecked the prospects for First World labor, especially in the US, while concentrating income and wealth in a few hands. Financial deregulation has resulted in lost private pensions and homelessness. The cost to the US Treasury of gratuitous wars and bank bailouts threatens the social safety net, Social Security and Medicare. Western democracy and civil liberties are endangered by authoritarian responses to protests against the austerity that is being imposed on citizens in order to fund wars and financial bailouts. Third World countries have had their economic development blocked by Western economic theories that do not reflect reality.

All of this is bad enough. But when we leave empty-world economics and enter the economics of a full-world, where nature's capital (natural resources) and ability to absorb wastes are being exhausted, we find ourselves in a worse situation. Even if countries are able to produce empty-world economic growth, economists cannot tell if the value of the increase in GDP is greater than its cost, because the cost of nature's capital is not included in the computation.

What does it mean to say that world GDP has increased four percent when the cost of nature's resources are not in the calculation?

Economist Herman Daly put it well when he wrote that the elites who make the decisions "have figured out how to keep the benefits for themselves while 'sharing' the costs with the poor, the future, and other species".[48]

Empty-world economics with its emphasis on spurring economic growth by the accumulation of man-made capital has run its course. Full-world economics is steady-state economics, and it is past time for economists to get to work on a new economics for a full world.

APPENDIX*

IS THE US ECONOMIC RECOVERY REAL?

In 2010 the National Bureau of Economic Research placed a 2009 date on recovery from the recession that began in December 2007.[49] The declared recovery is based on an upturn in GDP deflated with a measure that is believed to understate inflation by interpreting price increases as quality improvements. Statistician John Williams removes some of the nebulous hedonic quality adjustments to arrive at the corrected real GDP graph below. All other indicators—real retail sales, housing starts, consumer confidence, and payroll employment—indicate continuing recession.

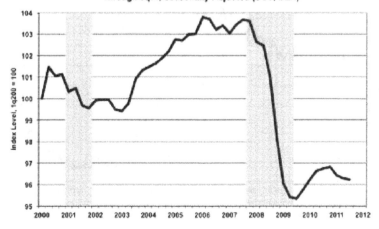

Inflation-Corrected Real GDP (Quarterly Index Level)
Through 3q11, Seasonally-Adjusted (SGS, BEA)

*The graphs are courtesy of John Williams (shadowstats.com).

Below is real retail sales:

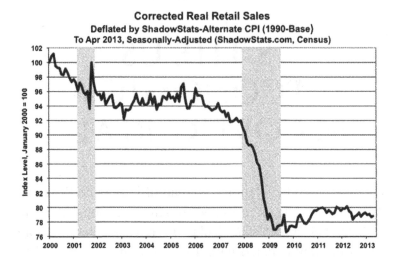

Below is housing starts:

Below is consumer confidence:

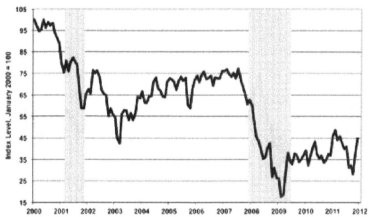

Below is nonfarm payroll employment:

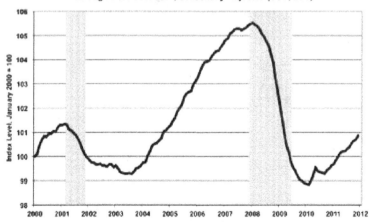

The graph below shows the difference in the measure of inflation by a constant basket of goods (top line) and the new substitution-based measure (bottom line):

The graph below shows average weekly earnings:

The graph below shows the US dollar's decline since 2001 in relation to gold and the Swiss franc:

Gold versus Swiss Franc
Monthly Average Price or Exchange Rate to April 2013
(ShadowStats.com, Kitco, FRB, WSJ)

ENDNOTES

Preface

1   Brasilien, Russland, Indien, China, Südafrika.

2   Paul Craig Roberts spielte bei der Durchsetzung dieser Politik im US-Kongress eine Schlüsselrolle – und veränderte damit weltweit die ökonomische Denkweise. In seinem spannenden Buch ‚The Supply-Side Revolution' (Harvard University Press) beschreibt Paul Craig Roberts die Hintergründe dieser Politik und die Kämpfe, die seinerzeit im US-Kongress stattfanden. The Supply-Side Revolution wird in Kürze in China in chinesischer Sprache veröffentlicht.

3   Der Begriff Reaganomics steht für die Wirtschaftspolitik des US-Präsidenten Ronald Reagan.

4   By liberal, Hayek and Maruschzik mean classical liberal, akin to today's libertarian, not postwar American liberals.

5   Allem voran gilt das für den Glass-Steagall Act, der 1933 verabschiedet wurde und die Fusion von Versicherungsgesellschaften, Investmentbanken und Geschäftsbanken verbot. Er wurde 1999 aufgehoben.

6   Forderungsbesicherte Schuldverschreibungen (Collateralized Debt Obligations / CDO) und besicherte Hypothekenobligationen (Collateralized Mortgage Obligations / CMO) spielten hier eine Schlüsselrolle.

7   Credit Default Swaps (CDS) sind Kreditderivate zum Handeln von Ausfallrisiken. Finanzinstitute verkauften sie, ohne Rücklagen für den Fall zu bilden, dass sie diese Art von ‚Versicherungen' an ihre Kunden auszahlen mussten. Der Commodity Futures Modernization Act hatte eine Regulierung der forderungsbesicherten Schuldverschreibungen und der CDS verhindert.

8   Siehe hierzu www.EconomyInCrisis.org

9   Siehe zum Beispiel http://www.nytimes.com/2012/06/12/business/

economy/family-net-worth-drops-to-level-of-early-90s-fed-says. html?_r=2

10 Matt Taibbi, Kleptopia. Wie uns die Finanzindustrie, Politik und Banken für dumm verkaufen. Seite 43.

11 Siehe ‚Das fatale Einheitsdenken in der EU. Lehren aus Selbsttäuschungen und Fehlschlägen', Jahrbuch ORDO, Band 62, 2011. Prof. Dr. Alfred Schüller war bis zur Emeritierung in 2005 Lehrstuhlinhaber und Geschäftsführender Direktor der Forschungsstelle zum Vergleich wirtschaftlicher Lenkungssysteme an der Philipps-Universität Marburg.

12 Legendär ist die Verordnung (EWG) Nr. 1677/88 (Gurkenverordnung), nach der die Krümmung bei Gurken der Handelsklasse ‚Extra' auf 10 cm Länge 10 mm nicht überschreiten durfte. Sie wurde 2009 wieder außer Kraft gesetzt.

13 Werner Plumpe, Wirtschaftskrisen – Geschichte und Gegenwart, Seite 103f.

14 Die jährliche Defizitquote (Haushaltsdefizit in Relation zum Bruttoinlandsprodukt / BIP) der einzelnen Mitgliedsstaaten der Eurozone sollte 3 % nicht übersteigen. Die Schuldenstandsquote (die zusammengefassten Staatsschulden in Relation zum BIP) der Länder sollte maximal 60 % erreichen.

15 ESM, Rechtliche und wirtschaftliche Analyse, Zusammenfassung und kritische Würdigung vom 14. Februar 2012, abrufbar unter http://www. taxpayers-europe.com/images/stories/ESM_-_Zusammenfassung__ und_kritische_Wrdigung_der_TAE.pdf

16 "Wir müssen in Athen mit anpacken" Interview mit Jean-Claude Juncker in der Tageszeitung Die Welt vom 29. Februar 2012.

17 Ein Hauptgrund für die Einführung des Euro war die Wiedervereinigung. Deutschland musste im Gegenzug die D-Mark und seine geldpolitische Souveränität aufgeben. Es gibt eine Vielzahl von Quellen, die das belegen. Siehe hierzu unter anderem Die Tragödie des €uro von Philipp Bagus.

18 The future of the euro. An economic perspective on the eurozone crisis. McKinsey Germany, January 2012, page 12.

The Failure of Laissez-Faire Capitalism

1 Paul Craig Roberts, *The Supply-Side Revolution*, Harvard University Press, 1984.

2 Paul Craig Roberts, Aldona Robbins, and Gary Robbins, "The Relative Impact of Taxation and Interest Rates on the Cost of Capital," in *Technology and Economic Policy*, edited by Ralph Landau and Dale Jorgenson, 1986.

3 See <http://healthimpactnews.com/2011/food-democracry-now-interviews-dr-don-huber-on-gmos-and-new-organism-that-threatens-u-s-agriculture/> and < http://www.fooddemocracynow.org/blog/2011/apr/6/don-hubers-cover-letter-euuk-commissions/>

4   See <http://www.opednews.com/articles/How-Did-This-Weedkiller-En-by-Sayer-Ji-111219-801.html>

5   <http://www.usgs.gov/newsroom/article.asp?ID=2909>

6   <http://www.alternet.org/story/153449/the_mysterious_death_of_dunkard_creek%3A_is_fracking_to_blame_for_one_of_the_worst_ecological_disasters_in_the_east>

7   See Herman Daly, *Ecological Economics and Sustainable Development*, U.K.: Edward Elgar Publishing, 2007.

8   See, for example, Michel Chossudovsky, *The Globalization of Poverty*, 2003, and the work of Michael Hudson especially *Trade, Development and Foreign Debt*, 2nd edition, 2009.

9   See, for example <http://www.informationclearinghouse.info/article29167.htm>

10   See, for example, <http://www.opednews.com/articles/How-the-Road-from-9-11-Led-by-Jess-Sundin-110908-814.html>

11   <http://www.wired.com/dangerroom/2011/09/fbi-muslims-radical/all/1>

12   See <http://www.opednews.com/populum/linkframe.php?linkid=137965>

13   <http://www.whitehouse.gov/sites/default/files/omb/legislative/sap/112/saps1867s_20111117.pdf>

14   <http://www.newyorker.com/online/blogs/comment/2012/05/the-presidents-kill-list.html>

15   See John Williams, shadowstats.com

16   <http://www.foxnews.com/us/2011/08/11/economic-woes-lead-to-proliferation-tent-cities-nationwide>

17   See, for example, this report: <http://www.guardian.co.uk/commentisfree/cifamerica/2011/sep/13/american-middle-class-poverty>

18   See <http://start.csail.mit.edu/mirror/cia.gov/library/publications/the-world-factbook/rankorder/2172rank.html>

19   See, for example, Francis Fukuyama, *The End of History*.

20   Patrick J. Buchanan, "The Fruits of Nafta", WND Commentary, March 10, 2006, <http://www.wnd.com/2006/03/35184/>

21   See <http://www.uscc.gov/hearings/2003hearings/transcripts/030925tran.pdf>

22   See < http://www.vdare.com/articles/charles-schumer-and-paul-craig-roberts-second-thoughts-on-free-trade-new-york-times-6-janua>

23   Alan S. Blinder, "Offshoring: The Next Industrial Revolution," Foreign Affairs, March-April 2006. < http://www.foreignaffairs.com/articles/61514/alan-s-blinder/offshoring-the-next-industrial-revolution>

24   Michael Mandel, "A Good Time to Learn Accounting?" Bloomberg Businessweek, March 9, 2005.<http://www.businessweek.com/the_thread/economicsunbound/archives/2005/09/good_time_to_le.html>

25   Shaheen Pasha, "The Outsourcing Wave Hits Investment Bankers," money.cnn.com, February 22, 2006. <http://money.cnn.com/2006/02/22/news/companies/banks_outsourcing/index.htm>

26   See <http://www.bls.gov/webapps/legacy/cesbtab1.htm>

27   See <http://www.bls.gov/webapps/legacy/cesbtab1.htm>

28   See <. http://www.bls.gov/news.release/ecopro.t06.htm>

29   See <http://nces.ed.gov/programs/digest/d04/tables/dt04_247.asp>

30   See <http://data.bls.gov/pdq/SurveyOutputServlet>

31   See <http://www.bls.gov/oes/2004/november/oes_15Co.htm>

32   Steve Lohr, "Outsourcing Is Climbing the Skills Ladder," *The New York Times*, February 16, 2006. <http://www.nytimes.com/2006/02/16/business/16outsource.html?ex=1297746000&en=fa39a3608333d562&ei=5090&partner=rssuserland&emc=rss&_r=1&>

33   See, for example, R. W. Thompson, *The History of Protective Tariff Laws* (Chicago: R.S. Peale, 1888) and Michael Hudson, America's Protectionist Takeoff, 1815-1914 (2010).

34   William Taussig, *The Tariff History of the United States* (New York: G.P. Putnam, 1914).

35   See <http://www.bea.gov/scb/pdf/2009/06%20June/0609_fdius.pdf >

36   See <http://www.bls.gov/opub/ted/2011/ted_20110224.htm   See also http://www.bls.gov/opub/mlr/2011/01/art3full.pdf >

37   Alan S. Blinder, *Dallas Morning News*, January 7, 2007.

38   See <http://www.cfr.org/industrial-policy/evolving-structure-american-economy-employment-challenge/p24366>

39   <https://cia.gov/library/publications/the-world-factbook/rankorder/2172rank.html>

40   See <http://www.nytimes.com/2011/09/14/us/14census.html?_r=1&hp>

41   See <http://www.informationweek.com/story/showArticle.jhtml?articleID=213000389>

42   See <http://english.pravda.ru/world/americas/107104-america_dominant_industry-0>

43   Manufacturing & Technology News, February 4, 2009.

44   http://www.marchandmeffre.com/detroit/

45   See <http://www.oecd.org/social/soc/41528678.pdf>

46   See <http://www.pbs.org/wgbh/pages/frontline/warning/view/>

47   See <http://www.statistics.gr/portal/page/portal/ESYE/BUCKET/A0704/PressReleases/A0704_SEL84_DT_QQ_04_2011_01_P_EN.pdf>

48   *Ecological Economics*, vol. 72, p. 8.

49   See <http://money.cnn.com/2010/09/20/news/economy/recession_over/index.htm>

INDEX

9/11 86-89

A

absolute advantage 36, 82, 121, 123, 155, 173
Afghanistan 88
Africa 131, 139, 171
AIG 147-149
Alfred P. Sloan Foundation 138
America 1, 17-18, 51, 55, 60, 65, 90, 96-99, 104-105, 107, 112-114, 117-120, 124-125, 127, 131-132, 134, 139, 142-144, 149, 156-157, 172
American COMPETES Act 138
American Immigration Lawyers Association 140
American Recovery and Reinvestment Act 143
Anderson, Martin 60
Anderson, Thomas 120
Asia 66, 131, 171
Assange, Julian 86
Augustine, Norm 104
austerity 75, 154, 157, 160
Austria 11, 101

B

Baiman, Ron 50
Ballmer, Steve 140
banksters 33, 146-147, 151-153
Barro, Robert 154-155
Baumol, William J. 47, 50-51, 126
Belgium 103
Berlusconi, Silvio 160
Bill of Rights 60

Blinder, Alan 102, 125-126
BLS (*see also* Bureau of Labor Statistics) 105-106, 110-111, 113, 117, 124
Born, Brooksley 32, 79, 151-153
Boyle, Francis A. 86
BP 59
Brazil 139
Brookings Institution 102
Buchanan, Patrick J. 99-100
budget deficit 19-20, 38-39, 43-45, 145, 158, 160, 166
Bureau of Economic Analysis (BEA) 120
Bureau of Labor Statistics (BLS) 53, 100, 103, 105, 110, 112, 121, 126, 128, 132
Bush, George W. 32, 49, 81, 85, 88-89, 94, 99, 107, 113, 117, 150, 152
Bush/Cheney regime 93
Business Roundtable 138
Business Week 56, 103, 150

C

Caesar 85, 94, 146
Cambodia 98
Cameroon 98
capital theory 42, 66
Carter administration 39, 42
Cassano, Joe 147-149
Caterpillar 143
CEOs 49, 70, 104, 116, 121, 127, 139-140, 145
Chemical & Engineering News 124
Chicago Sun-Times 104
China 11, 16, 19, 31, 43, 45-46, 49, 69, 75-77, 84, 94, 96, 98, 100-102,

104, 113, 115, 117, 120, 122-123,
131, 139
Chossudovsky, Michel 131
CIA 86, 89, 92-93, 134
Clark, Wesley 88
class war 83, 99
Cleveland 144
Clinton administration 32, 81, 85,
99, 133
Cobb, John B. 50
Cohen & Grigsby 136
Commodity Future Trading
Corporation (CFTC) 79, 151-153
comparative advantage 35, 47-49,
52, 82, 121
Computerworld 56
Conference Board 118
Congress 135, 137, 139, 151-153,
183
Consumer Price Index (CPI) 97
Council of Economic Advisers
Council on Competitiveness 118,
120, 122
Council on Foreign Relations 95,
128
Counterpunch 68
countervailing power 81
credit default swap 14, 32, 146-148,
168
current account deficit 53
Czech Republic 139

D

Daly, Herman E. 30, 50, 65, 70-71,
127, 174
Dawson County, Georgia 61
Dawsonville 61-62
debt monetization 45, 96, 145
Deloitte Touche 103
Delors, Jacques 170
democracy 83, 94, 161, 164-165,
171-172
Democrats 91, 113
Denmark 101
deregulation 1, 13-14, 32-34, 77-78,

98, 132, 158, 173
derivatives 103, 145-153
detainees 85, 92-93
Detroit 90, 144
discouraged workers 54, 132
dispossessed 1, 83-84
dollar 19-20, 26-27, 32, 44-46, 49,
53, 74, 80, 98, 117, 122, 126, 140,
145, 156-158, 169
Donohue, Thomas 143
Draghi, Mario 169-170

E

ecological economics 71
economic efficiency 79-81
economic growth 17, 27-29, 66-69,
71, 119, 173
economic planning 72
economic theory 12, 33ff, 96, 173
empty world economics 66, 70, 78,
173-174
enemy combatants 85
Engdahl, William 68
Environmental Protection Agency
(EPA) 59
euro 16, 19-20, 23-24, 26-28, 80,
163, 168-169
Europe 14, 16, 19-22, 24-29, 31, 34,
76, 78, 83, 115, 128, 161, 164,
168-169, 171-172
European Central Bank (ECB) 24,
154, 159-161, 163, 167-170
European Union (EU) 23, 34, 96,
159, 161, 164-166, 168, 170
executive branch 17, 85, 92-93
external cost 54, 60

F

Farley, J. 71
FBI 86-87, 89-91
Federal Reserve 13, 20, 32-33, 38,
42, 45-46, 62, 79, 96102, 125,
133, 149, 151-154, 158, 169
Feldstein, Martin 157

First World 31, 69, 75-77, 99, 101, 109, 127, 131, 173
Flint, Michigan 144
Florida Hometown Democracy 63
Ford, Henry 140
foreign direct investment 119-120
Foreign Intelligence Surveillance Act (FISA) 85
fracking 29, 60, 68
Frank, Robert 144
free trade 1, 13-14, 33, 35-36, 47, 49-53, 66-67, 76, 78, 82, 102, 116, 121, 126-127, 143, 155
Friedman, Milton 35, 38
full world economics 66, 70, 74, 78, 173-174

G

Galbraith, James K. 50
Gary, Indiana 144, 153
Gates, Bill 139
GDP (*see also* gross domestic product) 33, 43-44, 46, 52, 94, 118, 123, 133-134, 155 -156, 166, 168, 173-175
Geithner, Timothy 153
General Electric 143
Geneva Conventions 85, 92-93
Gensler, Gary 153
Georgescu-Roegen, Nichoas 67
Giavazzi, Francesco 154
Gini index 134
Glass-Steagall Act 14, 146
Global Research 68
globalism 13, 15, 26, 34, 69-70, 75, 110, 112, 117-119, 127-128, 130-132, 134, 155, 158
GMOs 58-59
GNP 166
gold 38-39, 46, 179
Goldman Sachs 18, 149, 152-153, 159, 169-170
Goldsmith, Sir James 127-128, 130
Gomory, Ralph E. 47, 50-51, 126-128

Grassley, Charles 55, 140, 142-143
Great Depression 14, 37-38, 140, 143, 156
Greece 83, 125, 160-164, 166-168, 170
Greenspan, Alan 13, 62, 79, 150-154
Griffiths, Lord 153
gross domestic product (GDP) 33, 43-44, 46, 52, 94, 118, 123, 133-134, 155-156, 166, 168, 173-175
Gulf of Mexico 59, 63, 66
Gutierrez, Carlos 113

H

H-1B work visas 55-56, 97, 107-108, 110, 114, 135-136, 139-142
habeas corpus 85
Heckscher-Ohlin 75-77
Hitler, Adolf 88
Hlatshwayo, Sandile 128
Homeland Security 85, 89-90
Hong Kong 150
Horn, Steve 68
House Science Committee 113
Huber, Don 58-59
Hudson, Michael 1, 50, 161
human mapping program 86

I

IBM 56, 139
income distribution 98, 117, 130, 134-135, 153
income inequality 69, 121, 150-151
India 31, 56-57, 69, 75-77, 84, 90, 94, 96, 101, 103-104, 113, 115, 117, 120, 123, 126, 131, 137, 139-140
Infosys 56
Innovation 52, 114-115, 124
Intel 139
International Monetary Fund (IMF) 45, 75-76, 160-162, 166-167
Iran 88, 98
Iraq 88
Italy 83, 125, 161, 168-170

J

jobs offshoring 1, 94-95, 102, 105, 110, 112, 119, 124, 126, 130, 142-145, 151
Jordan 98
Journal of Monetary Economics 80
JPMorgan Chase 56

K

Kennedy, John F. 69, 134
Kenya 98
Keynes, John Maynard 35, 166
Keynesian 12, 37-40, 42-43, 154-155
Kobe, Kathryn 124
Krugman, Paul 154-155

L

labor arbitrage 15, 82, 100, 121, 131
labor compensation 100, 121
laissez faire 13, 37, 74, 78
Latin America 131
Lebowitz, Lawrence 136
Levin, Carl 92
Levitt, Arthur 79, 151-152
Libya 88
Lorenz curve 134
losses 11, 13, 15-16, 34, 53, 59, 84, 96, 100, 109, 161-162, 167, 169

M

macroeconomics 12, 35, 37, 39-40, 42-43
Mandel, Michael 103
man-made capital 13, 29, 66-67, 74, 174
Manning, Bradley 86
Manufacturing & Technology News 100
manufacturing 15-17, 31, 46, 53, 77, 81, 95-96, 100-102, 104, 106-110, 112, 114-118, 120, 123, 124, 142-144

Marshall, Alfred 35, 36, 42, 70
Marx, Karl 71-72, 96
Matloff, Norm 103, 136
McCain, John 143
McDonald's 57, 104
McMillion, Charles 127-128, 130
median household income 97, 135
Merkel, Angela 24, 160, 165
Mexico 59, 63-64, 66, 139
microeconomics 40
Microsoft 139-142
military detention 92-93
Miller, Janice 56
Milliken, Roger 127-128, 130
monetarism 35, 43
Monsanto 59
Monti, Mario 25, 170
Morgenson, Gretchen 146
Morici, Peter 44
Motorola 139
Muslim 87-88, 90

N

NAFTA 99
Namibia 134
National Academies 115, 138
National Association of Manufacturers 124, 143
National Center for Education Statistics 110-111
National Defense Authorization Act 91, 93
National Economic Council 143, 153
nature's capital 13, 29-30, 66-68, 74, 173
Neuger, Win 148-149
New Economy 131, 151
New York Times 56, 115, 154, 163
Nicaragua 98
Nielsen Company 56
Nigeria 60, 98, 139
Nixon, Richard 84
nontradable domestic service jobs 102, 107, 11053,
Nordhaus, William 67

Norway 101

O

Obama administration 81, 85
Obama regime 86-88, 92-94, 107
Occupational Employment Statistics
  113, 117
Occupy Wall Street movement 83
offshored production 46, 49, 52-53,
  100, 142
opportunity cost 41, 47-48
Organization for Economic Co-
  operation and Development
  (OECD) 150-151
Orlov, Dmitry 72-73
OTC derivatives 150-152

P

Pagano, Marco 154
Papademos, Lucan 170
Papandreou, George 160, 163
Pasha, Shaheen 103
PATRIOT Act 85
payroll jobs 105, 114, 117
performance pay 46
Perot, Ross 99-100
PIIGS 159, 162, 165
Pittsburgh 144
Polanyi, Michael 38
police state 17, 83, 88, 90-91, 94
pollution 29, 60, 65, 68
Popkin, Joel 124
population 11, 13, 16, 39, 43, 56, 66,
  68-69, 74-75, 88-89, 96, 98, 105,
  112, 123, 132, 144, 156, 160, 163,
  171
Porter, Michael 118-120, 122-126
position limits 149
Posse Comitatus Act 92
Prasch, Robert E. 50
Pravda 142
production function 29, 67, 102
productivity growth 120-121
profit maximization 78, 82

profits 32, 36, 42, 47, 49, 53, 61-62,
  64, 68, 73, 76-78, 82, 95-98, 123,
  130, 142, 147, 152, 155, 167
property rights 61-63, 80
public debt 33, 80, 159-160

Q

Quantitative Easing (QE) 45-46

R

Raimondo, Justin 86
Reagan administration 12, 28, 42,
  54, 81, 95, 98, 119, 134, 151, 157
Reagan, Ronald 54, 81, 95, 98, 129,
  134, 151, 157
regulation 132, 146, 149, 151-152,
  158, 173
relative prices 40-41
Republicans 91, 113
research and development (R&D)
  103, 114-115, 124-125, 156
reserve currency 18-19, 27, 44-46,
  74, 80, 84, 117, 119, 126, 145, 156
Ricardo, David 14, 35, 47-48, 50-52
Richistan 144-145
Roach, Stephen 104
robber barons 81
Rochester, New York 144
Roemer, Buddy 100
Rosner, Joshua 146
Roundup 59
Rubin, Robert 79, 151-153
Russia 11, 28, 34, 45, 72, 88, 96,
  139, 171-172

S

Samuelson, Paul 37, 40, 50, 76
Sanders, Bernie 55, 140
Sarkozy, Nicolas 161
Satyam 56
securitization 146
Senegal 98
shadowstats.com 97, 132, 175

short-selling 148
Shultz, George 154
silver 46
Singapore 150
Slaughter, Matthew J. 117
Smith, Adam 35, 64, 70
social costs 15, 58, 65, 69, 80
Solow, Robert 29, 67
South Africa 139
South Bend, Indiana 144
sovereign debt crisis 20-21, 29, 158-160, 167-169
sovereignty 20, 24-25, 28, 34, 159, 163-164
Soviet Union 31, 34, 36, 71-73, 82
Spain 59, 83, 125, 161, 168-169
Spence, Michael 95, 128, 130-131
Spiegleman, Matthew 118
Sprint Nextel 139
St. Louis, Missouri 144
Stalin, Joseph 88-89, 91
steady-state economics 68-69, 174
Stigler, George 58
Stiglitz, Joseph 29, 67
stimulus debate 154-155, 158
Storch, Adam 153
Summers, Larry 79, 151-153
Sunstein, Cass 86
supply-side economics 28, 35, 40, 42-43, 119
Supreme Court 18, 84
Sweden 134

T

Taibbi, Matt 18, 146-148, 149
Tata 56
Taussig, Frank William 116
Teitelbaum, Michael S. 138-139
terrorist threat 85
Texas Instruments 139
Thailand 98
Thatcher, Margaret 41
The Failure Of Laissez Faire Capitalism
The International Economy 154

Third World 97-98, 102, 110, 112, 126, 131, 167, 173
Thompson, R.W. 51
Tobin, James 67
tradable goods 47-48, 53-54, 66, 102, 115, 124, 130
tradable services 54, 114, 124-126, 130
trade deficit 43-44, 46, 53, 95, 108, 116, 120, 122, 126, 156, 167
Trichet, Jean-Claude 25, 154, 164-165, 168
Troubled Asset Relief Program (TARP) 140, 149, 152
Turkmenistan 98

U

U.S. Census Bureau 134-135, 144
U.S. Chamber of Commerce 105, 140, 143
U.S. Constitution 17, 83-85, 87-88, 92-93
U.S. Department of Labor 107-108, 121
U.S. Treasury 152-153, 164, 173, 183
U.S.-China Commission 102
undeclared agenda 91, 165
United Arab Emirates 139
United Nations Development Program 150
United States 12, 16-20, 22, 27-28, 49, 51, 57, 88-89, 92-94, 98, 101, 113, 115-123, 126, 128-130, 132, 144, 157, 172
Uruguay 98
USA Today 139

V

Van Rompuy, Herman 169
Volcker, Paul 42, 154

W

Wall Street 27, 31, 49, 68, 80-81, 83-
    84, 103, 116, 128, 146-148, 150,
    152, 155, 159, 164
Walton County, Florida 62
war on terror 85, 94
wealth distribution 84, 150
wealth inequality 70, 121, 150-151,
    163
Wikileaks 86
Williams, John 97, 132-133, 175
Wipro 56
Wired 87

Z

Zandi, Mark 154
zoning 62

PAUL CRAIG ROBERTS

The Honorable Dr. Roberts was educated at Georgia Tech, the University of Virginia, the University of California, Berkeley, and Oxford University where he was a member of Merton College.

He was Assistant Secretary of the US Treasury in the Reagan administration, a member of the US Congressional staff, associate editor and columnist for the *Wall Street Journal*, columnist for *Business Week*, the Scripps Howard News Service, and Creators Syndicate, Senior Research Fellow, Hoover Institution, Stanford University, and was appointed to the William E. Simon Chair in Political Economy, Center for Strategic and International Studies, Georgetown University.

He is chairman of the Institute for Political Economy and author or coauthor of ten books and numerous articles in scholarly journals. He has testified before committees of Congress on 30 occasions.

Dr. Roberts was awarded the US Treasury's Meritorious Service Award for "outstanding contributions to the formulation of US economic policy," and France's Legion of Honor as "the artisan of a renewal in economic science and policy after half a century of state interventionism."

To learn more about Dr. Paul Craig Roberts visit his website at: http://www.paulcraigroberts.com.